NEGRI ON NEGRI

NEGRI ON NEGRI

ANTONIO NEGRI

WITH ANNE DUFOURMANTELLE

TRANSLATED BY M. B. DEBEVOISE

ROUTLEDGE
NEW YORK AND LONDON

Published in 2004 by
Routledge
29 West 35th Street
New York, NY 10001
www.routledge-ny.com

Published in Great Britain by
Routledge
11 New Fetter Lane
London EC4P 4EE
www.routledge.co.uk

Printed in the United States of America on acid-free paper.

10 9 8 7 6 5 4 3 2 1

Ouvrage publié avec le concours du Ministère français chargé de la Culture—
Centre National du Livre

Originally published as Duretour: Abécé-daire biopolitique, © Calman-Levy, 2002

Library of Congress Cataloging-in-Publication Data

Negri, Antonio, 1933-
    [Du retour. English]
    Negri on Negri / Antonio Negri with Anne Dufourmantelle ; translated by
M. B. DeBevoise.
        p. cm.
Includes bibligraphical references and index.
    ISBN 0-415-96894-1 (HB) — ISBN 0-415-96895-X (PB)
    1. Communism—Italy. 2. World politics—20th century. 3. Political science. I.
Dufourmantelle, Anne. II. Title.
    HX289.N374L3 2004
    335. 43'092—dc22   2003022839

CONTENTS

v

INTRODUCTION

ANNE DUFOURMANTELLE: I propose that we collaborate on a biographical and biopolitical abecedary, isolating words for each letter that have a particular meaning for you—thus, for example, A as in Arms, B as in Brigate Rosse, *C as in Camp, and so on.*

ANTONIO NEGRI: This would be a departure from the familiar conventions of the interview—and one that would give it a certain liveliness! It may also permit me to express myself in a new way, and to address topics I've never talked about before.

Since your thought is highly structured, this alphabetical device might serve to introduce a musical counterpoint.

I don't know if I'd be capable of anything musical. But there is a sort of polyphonic motif that I've been living with for a long time, the motif of return, which is now at the center of my biography. This return has had different meanings: the first, quite obviously, has been that of a physical return to Italy after fourteen years of exile—and therefore in prison after fourteen years of liberty; a dramatic return that once again put my whole life at stake. But there has also been another return, another meaning that was both intellectual and political: I reintegrated myself into the *vita activa.* Exile, even when it is extremely active—as mine had been—is draining. I lived for fourteen years without papers. It's hard to make others understand how difficult it is to get by, how much of a void this type of life ends up creating. In coming back to Italy, even if I am deprived of my civil rights and forbidden to hold public office, I nonetheless have the feeling of being a citizen. In this new situation, I am able to think of my experience as having been enriched by exile: I bring to the current debate a prior life that hasn't been frustrated by the sense of failure that many of my comrades experienced after the catastrophic outcome of the 1970s and 1980s. Today there is a renewed hope of transforming ourselves and transforming the world, and so, ingenuously perhaps, I continue to believe in the power of another revolutionary moment. I recall Machiavelli when he speaks in the *Discourses* of political and religious bodies, and affirms that "those changes make for their conservation which lead them back to their origins."[1] And, after having noted how much constituent activity is required to maintain republics, he adds that the necessity of such "renovations" is no less clear from "the example of our own religion, which, if it had not been restored to its starting point by Saint Francis and Saint Dominic, would have become quite extinct."[2] This renewal is—return! Physical return is also a return to the physical passion of the past, to the renewal of the spirit.

And so it remains for us only to set out on our way, going back to the past in order to discover in it the themes of the present.

---

1. Niccolò Machiavelli, *The Discourses*, edited with an introduction by Bernard Crick, using the translation of Leslie J. Walker, with revisions by Brian Richardson (New York: Penguin, 1998), 385.
2. Ibid., 389.

A AS IN . . .

Perhaps we might begin with A as in Arms. How did the armed struggle begin?

There was such a desire for liberation—but this desire found itself confronted by a systematic state terrorism that planted bombs, that killed people, that practiced repression. It is now known that the first terrorist acts were planned by the state. State-sponsored terrorism was based on fear. And the construction of fear was based on the government's fear of the masses, which it imposed upon the masses to prevent unrest, exactly as Spinoza remarked in the *Tractatus Theologico-Politicus.*

It is too often forgotten that Europe was in the midst of the Cold War.

The Italian government would never have dared to act in this way if it hadn't enjoyed the legitimacy given it by the anticommunist climate of the period, and the tension of the Cold War. Italy is this strange, very long country that stretches toward the Mediterranean. . . .

What would have happened if the regime in Italy had changed during the Cold War? The Communist party in Italy was so important—it was the party of the Resistance, the only one that had really been antifascist. After 1968 Berlinguer was the head of the Communist party. He had said that even if the party got 51 percent of the vote he would refuse to form a government. This was after Chile: he absolutely did not want to play the game any more. On the one hand there had been Yugoslavia; on the other the Mediterranean, Israel, and Palestine. It was an explosive situation.

At the time everyone knew that the first major attack, the Piazza Fontana bombing in Milan, in December 1969, was *una strage di Stato*—a massacre of state. Still today poor Adriano Sofri is in prison for that, having been accused of having the chief of police in Milan killed by his political group, Lotta Continua.[3] This execution was alleged to have been carried out to avenge the death of an anarchist named Pinelli who had been arrested by the police following the attacks. Pinelli, of course,

---

3. Adriano Sofri was one of the leaders of the extraparliamentary group Lotta Continua. On December 12, 1969 a bomb exploded in the main hall of the Banca Nazionale dell'Agricoltura in the heart of Milan, in the Piazza Fontana, killing seventeen people and wounding eighty-eight (note continued on page 30)

had nothing to do with the Piazza Fontana bombing, but he "fell" from an upper-story window of the police station under shadowy circumstances that remain unclear. These are typically Italian stories, but one has to try to imagine the climate that prevailed at the time. In short, it is true that there was terrorism in Italy; but terrorism began with the terrorism of the state. The Piazza Fontana bombing at the end of 1969 ushered in a new period.

Why?

When the police said that it was an anarchist attack, nobody believed them. Today the courts themselves believe that the CIA was involved, even the Italian secret services; and that the state—diverted from its true purpose, yes, but nonetheless the state—was behind all this. In Italy, if you look at the reports of the parliamentary commissions charged with investigating the Piazza Fontana bombing, or the bombing in the Piazza della Loggia in Brescia, or the *Italicus* train bombing, you always arrive at the same conclusions.

Why, then, did the government embark upon this course of action? To create terror. And why create terror? Italy was governed by the Christian Democrats: a country on the edge of Western Europe with a Communist party and other left-wing parties that together accounted for 35 percent of the vote—a completely uncontrollable social dynamic. But there was also an obvious modernity in the conception of labor not only as material labor but also as intellectual labor, in the rejection of wage labor—themes that still, thirty years later, constitute the daily bread of sociologists and economists.

And so the people organized themselves in response to this violence. But was it necessary to respond with terrorism to these terrorist acts, which you maintain were sponsored by the state? Was there no alternative?

The response that was given was not at first a terrorist response, but an extremist response. It was necessary to respond at the same level that had been imposed by the police actions of the state. The first military actions began three or four years after the Milan bombing, in 1973 or 1974.

Fairly late, then—

No one has ever shown that there were infiltrations—it was spontaneous. Confronted with the increasing violence of the forces of order, the people who were demonstrating began to arm themselves in self-defense. The repression by the state operated on all levels: in the factory, in the street, everywhere. There had been innumerable layoffs. The extremists responded militarily because all other responses had become impossible. Then there came a very difficult moment in 1977: the September demonstrations in Bologna.[4] There were tanks in the city. French

---

4. In the wake of large and spontaneous demonstrations in Bologna and Rome during the spring of 1977—which ended, particularly in Bologna, in violent repression, the shutting down of the main independent radio station of the movement (Radio Alice), the entry of tanks into the very center of Bologna and the encircling of the university quarter, and the deaths of several demonstrators in both Bologna and Rome—a group of French intellectuals organized a conference in Bologna the following September. Foucault, Deleuze, Guattari, and others defended the need for an Italian "political laboratory" and sharply criticized the violence of the state.

intellectuals came to Italy—Deleuze, Foucault, the whole intellectual Left that was opposed to the repression taking place.

Were you able at the time to imagine a nonviolent response?

No, absolutely not. We, too, were organized. The only thing we hadn't anticipated was that the state would resort to Stalinist techniques. This began with the arrest of dozens of leaders of the extreme Left, on April 7, 1979, which led to what came to be known as the Sette Aprile trial.

What happened that day?

We were arrested—myself and some sixty others, almost all of us academics. They struck at the intellectuals within the "movement" with incredible accusations—"armed insurrection against the state," for example. For a long time the sentence for this kind of thing had been the death penalty! Fortunately, with the constitution of 1948, the death penalty had been replaced by a life sentence. Still, it was incredible and terrifying. We laughed, we couldn't believe it, but it was terrible just the same. Paradoxically, the extreme Left found itself caught between the Christian Democrats, the party of the bourgeoisie, and the Communist party! The Communist party considered us uncontrollable and therefore dangerous. Some feared that we would form a separate party.

The Communist party attacked you in the name of what?

In the name of the nation, or, more precisely, the Treaty of Yalta, which is to say the willingness to align oneself with the Soviets. It is this logic that we rejected: it meant having to defer to the Party and allowing it to go on cultivating its singularity. But this singularity wasn't defensible.

You were defending Communist ideas, then, not the Communist party?

We were absolutely opposed to totalitarianism in any form. We were seeking a true redistribution of wealth. It is almost impossible to live decently if one isn't able to study, to work: society must be organized in such a way that people have these rights. This isn't really a very utopian dream—the paradox is that many of the ideas that we advanced were later adopted by advanced capitalism!

The problem is that government, in order to make the job of managing society easier, invents increasingly elaborate disciplinary procedures. We offered to take over this management role because we were searching for a real transformation of social relations. And it was this offer that the Italian authorities turned down so harshly.

And so you found yourself abandoned on both sides.

The Communist party taught the Christian Democrats the usefulness of Stalinist trials—absolute condemnation, eliminating one's enemies, crushing them. Outrageous arguments were employed, depraved modes of reasoning. In my case I had, it is true, written revolutionary things that the authorities judged dangerous. Therefore I had to have been in contact with those who did "dangerous things." Therefore I was also the head of a criminal conspiracy. And to the extent that I was the head of a "subversive" political group, all my close friends and associates were necessarily members of this group. Thus it came about, for example, that I found myself in prison with a friend whom I hadn't seen for ten years: a miracle of surreal logic! There was no limit to "preventive" incarceration. Most of those who were accused in the Sette Aprile trial ended up being released, but not before they had spent six or seven years in prison under preventive detention, waiting for a trial that never came. Six or seven years for nothing. And not a word of apology. I was fortunate to have been elected a parliamentary deputy after four years in a maximum-security prison, and so I was able to get out. Two months later there was a great debate in the Chamber of Deputies over whether my parliamentary immunity should be revoked, and I lost by a vote of 300–296. Those four votes would have sent me back to prison. The situation was so tense that I feared for my life, and I decided to leave for France. All on account of four votes. . . .

They let you leave the country?

No, I escaped. But I always thought that they let me get out because, of course, they had informers, and if they'd wanted to prevent me from leaving they certainly could have done so. The paradox is that the decisive four votes were cast by members of the Radical party, which had put me up as a candidate on its lists to get me out of prison. Three months later they sentenced me to go back.

If you had not been elected, you would have remained in prison like the others.

I imagine I'd still be there, yes.

Like Adriano Sofri.

Sofri went to prison only four years ago. He had been arrested at the same time I was, but not for the same reason. And ten years ago he was arrested again. This whole business was organized as an act of revenge: Sofri found himself once again accused of arranging the assassination of the police superintendent involved in the defenestration of the anarchist accused in the Piazza Fontana bombing. The anarchist, Pinelli, had nothing to do with that, but he was dead. In the meantime the superintendent, who was named Calabresi, had been shot down by gunmen. The courts then charged Sofri's organization, Lotta Continua, on the basis of accusations made in the 1980s—much later, then—by a very dubious "penitent" who had been an active member of Lotta Continua. The whole affair caused an enormous stir in Italy, a great many signatures calling for Sofri's release were collected—but there was nothing to be done. He was sentenced, just like the other former members of Lotta Continua, to twenty-two years in prison, and has been incarcerated since February 1997. All this is absurd. How can I explain it to you? Mechanisms of vengeance have been employed by the police in France as well, and these mechanisms are particularly formidable when one of their own is involved. Someone has to pay.

Is it true that the Red Brigades never forgave you for leaving for France?

No—the Red Brigades wanted me to declare that the war was over.

The war against the state?

Yes. A decision had to be made. It's a long story. . . .

I knew certain members of the Red Brigades, and so I had an inside view of the movement's formation—I even had a certain sympathy for it, at the very beginning. Together with a few members of the Red Brigades I was one of the founders of a journal called *Contro-informazione.* But then they began to kill. Obviously I no longer endorsed their actions! There were many other comrades whom I was in contact with who rejected this strategy as well. And so we said publicly that we did not agree with it. Moreover, the first assassination committed by the Red Brigades was purely accidental—the theory came afterward, it was absurd. The assassination occurred in Padua, at the university, where I was teaching at the time: they attacked the offices of the Fascist party, and a *carabiniere*—a policeman who had infiltrated their group—opened fire on them. They killed him. There was no intention to assassinate anyone, it was an act of self-defense; but the leadership of the Red Brigades decided that it was absolutely necessary to explain this murder by giving it a theoretical justification. From that moment on they acted irrationally. The most serious moment, of course, was the Aldo Moro affair. We did everything we could to save Moro's life. We even went to speak with a member of the government, Bettino Craxi, who was then the head of the Socialist party—we felt that that the armed struggle had reached a point of no return and that it was absolutely necessary to save Moro. The Red Brigades had to be stopped. A year later we tried to isolate the Red Brigades in the factories. It was then that the state took the initiative and decided to "deprive the fish of the water in which they swam"—that was the image they used! To make a long story short, we were the ones who were arrested. We later found ourselves in prison with the very people in the Red Brigades whom we had tried to reason with. These were special prisons—we were all thrown together, which made it easier for us to be lumped together in the public mind. It was convenient for the authorities: I was accused of being the head of the Red Brigades, and so the "movement" was decapitated. . . .

Was it at this moment that you said that the armed struggle was finished?

In 1981 I was one of ninety prisoners at Trani who issued a statement—the "Document of the 90," as it was known—saying just this. It declared that the armed struggle was over, and that all those who pursued it in the future would be considered enemies. The response of the Red Brigades was to say that they were going to kill us. And, of course, they were going to begin with me. It was a death sentence. When I came back to Italy, in July 1997, I was put into a cell with the man who was ordered to kill me! It was amusing to see that the authorities were still trying to toy with us, even though twenty years had passed and that none of that any longer had any meaning. The man assigned to eliminate me has since become a good friend—together we have established a cooperative to help prisoners when they get out. There are still dozens of *brigatisti* in prison, many of them for life. A few have become very dear friends.

What do they say now?

That I've remained a communist and they haven't! Sometimes we talk about that period. They've all changed—a life sentence leaves time to reflect, but also to make other choices, to learn, to study, to choose a trade. And so to go on keeping them in prison, at this late date, really no longer makes any sense, unless it is purely and simply a matter of vengeance. One of my cellmates is now the head of an enormous advertising company in Rome, and this has been his life for the ten years that he has been granted partial liberty. He built up the business himself and has been very successful: at night he sleeps in prison; the next day he turns into a brilliant businessman. When I was subject to the same regime we used to leave in the morning and come back together in the evening. It was a bit like a boarding school—at night we traded stories of what we'd done during the day.

And this man who was supposed to kill you, he never really thought about it, until—

No—it's rather odd, but that's how it was. He's a gentleman, you see. When he speaks about the past now, he finds the whole thing crazy—he doesn't understand. I believe that for people like him it was, in fact, a totally schizophrenic experience. He remained a man of the Left, but others veered to the Right. At the beginning we talked a great deal, because there were six of us in the cell. We talked all the time. Later there was just two of us, and at night we often went to sleep after watching a little television. The ex-Red Brigades member who went into advertising told me an incredible story, funny and sad at the same time, that goes back to 1982, which is to say to the last stages of the armed struggle. He was part of the commando team that abducted an American general, Dozier, an important NATO official.[5] Each member of the commando team had a specific responsibility. His job was to go to Dozier's home, restrain him, put him in a crate, and hand it over to the others. When he'd finished doing his part he found himself all alone and suddenly realized how absurd the whole thing was. He'd wanted simply to be an ordinary thief, not a revolutionary—so he pocketed the general's war medals and his wife's jewelry, without, of course, saying anything to the other *brigatisti*. In reality the Red Brigades had reached a moment of crisis—its time had passed and he knew it, and so stealing the jewelry and medals amounted in a way to an act of survival! Eventually the case went

---

5. Brigadier General James L. Dozier, senior American officer at the NATO base in Verona, was abducted by the Red Brigades in December 1981—a moment when the "movement" had been decapitated by a campaign of repression and massive arrests, provoking an increasingly violent response from small armed groups. Dozier was freed by the police shortly afterward.

to trial and they were all sentenced to life, but he was given three months extra for "aggravated theft." The others, learning all this in the courtroom, were stunned. Prison is full of terrible stories like this that are both comic and tragic.

It needs also to be pointed out that stealing was a real transgression, because in general the *brigatisti* lived in real poverty. They all received a worker's salary, the minimum wage authorized by the revolutionary party; but living underground was difficult, and their expenses were exorbitant. They lived in total destitution, ready to flee at any moment, moving from one apartment to another. And so to steal jewelry because one is faced with a political crisis and dreams only of being, just once, a common, small-time criminal. . . .

Not all the members of the Red Brigades were arrested.

No—almost all of them, except for the ones who had gone to France, and a few others who were in Brazil, England, Central America. But the rest were all arrested.

In short, from the moment that we signed the "Document of the 90," the rupture was complete, even in prison. We declared a policy of total separation with regard to the armed struggle. This policy went into effect in 1981–82, and the *brigatisti* ended up abandoning the struggle in 1986. On Christmas Day in 1980 there had been a revolt in the special prison we were in at Trani. It was put down with such violence that we quickly came to the conclusion there was no point carrying on. Renouncing armed struggle and no longer recognizing actions that were taken outside prison was called "dissociation."

The second reason why the armed struggle lasted so long in Italy has to do with a certain communist tradition anchored in the memory of resistance to fascism during the Second World War. There was a very strong historical homogeneity between the movement for liberation and the postwar socialist struggles. The antifascist resistance had spread throughout the various regions of the north of Italy. Catholicism also found itself shaken, and the great crisis of Catholicism, with John XXIII, was a response to the sudden changes in values and the economy confronted by parish priests in the north. In the small communities formed by the young in Italy, after 1968, there were two problems: resistance to the capitalist colonialization of life on the one hand, and the emergence of a model of intellectual labor on the other—these in addition to the communist tradition of class struggle and the problem of internal immigration. All this led to a radicalization of the struggles, which is to say a "class war." What happened following 1968 was therefore perceived as a resumption of wartime resistance. This is probably also why it lasted for ten years, and not a few weeks as elsewhere, which had the effect of strengthening the movement's capacity for reform. Italy was the first country where the struggles did not take place in the factory but permeated society as a whole: there were demands for the "autoreduction" of rents and the cost of public transport tickets, for example—one struggled for a better life. In Milan, where I lived a good part of the 1970s, there were neighborhoods that had been "liberated" and where neither taxes, nor transport charges, nor rents were paid—

"Self-managed" neighborhoods?

Yes, self-managed. These were neighborhoods where another form of organization could be experimented with. The joy there was amazing. If the police came into the neighborhood, they were immediately expelled. All available houses were occupied— empty apartments were taken over and inhabited. I lived on the edge of one of these neighborhoods. It was an incredible life, unimaginable.

Let's come back to the Trani revolt.

It was a special prison, a maximum-security wing for political prisoners where we were all confined. There was a revolt, the guards were taken prisoner, we barricaded ourselves in the prison for three days. The police came and attacked. It was war. So we resisted by overturning garbage cans, smashing the pipes and flooding the buildings, knocking down the walls, and arming ourselves by all possible means. Think of American films, it was just like that. Later, when the revolt had been put down—bombs were dropped from helicopters—the police beat us bloody, one after another. There were episodes of torture. We were thirty to a cell, and from time to time the guards came in. . . .

All that was very hard. I've never been a romantic in politics. It is true that the extremists became terrorists. But I must say that in spite of everything I came out of all these situations with a certain—confidence. I have always considered political assassi- nation a crime, and therefore something that has to be resisted. I think that the Red Brigades, who were extremists to begin with, became terrorists because they were forced to become terrorists. The relation of forces at the time left no alternative for the most part. The only hope of really winning lay in forming a political party, an organization, a movement. This is what we had tried to do, but patience was required, even if the terrorism of the state pushed us out of control. In prison we realized that peace had to be negotiated—

And that the romantic view of having to choose between all and nothing had to be abandoned?

It was necessary to find a way out of this impasse, and events pointed in this direction. Today all that is over, except in certain very hard-core Stalinist circles. After that my problem was to find a way to get out of prison. When I was elected a deputy I was freed, thanks to my parliamentary immunity; but then there was a movement to strip me of this immunity. When it became clear that I would be going back to jail I fled to France. I waited until the parliamentary battle was over to make up my mind, but I knew all along that they wanted to put me back in prison. No one could accept an open alternative. I had to be put back in the legal system, in the maze of the judiciary. Very often in Italy it all comes down to this. Judicial power is now virtually unchecked. At the time one was witnessing the emergence of a society of judges whose authority had become excessive because it derived from agreements with the political Left. The people of the Left realized that they could do anything they wanted. Mind you, I am convinced that a legal system is absolutely necessary. The tragedy is when it takes over the political space and comes to dictate its laws. What was done against the extreme Left in the late 1970s was done again ten years later by the judges against the

Socialists and Berlusconi's followers. It's rather amusing, this backlash.

I therefore decided to flee. This represented a second laceration, having to tear myself away from my friends, from all those who remained in prison. My justification for doing this was, I believe, quite reasonable: "If I stay with all of you, in prison, you stay with me, and they will keep you there for years; if I go away, you will be freed." This is what happened.

At the same moment there was a general crisis in Italy, above all an economic crisis, that was causing an enormous transformation—the transformation that we've been trying to describe since the 1970s. If you go to the Veneto region today, you will find heads of companies who were "red" workers and who have become heads of small businesses. The whole capitalist transformation of the 1980s is now visible. Politically, these new bosses remain unchanged in one sense: they may have gotten rich, but they still despise money. They weren't allowed to pursue their struggles to the end, however, so they were forced to bring about the transformation of production by other means—a transformation they had foreseen more clearly than others, since it was precisely for this that they were fighting. This is an odd end to the story.

In Italy, in any case, one thing is certain: the chance of modernizing politics was lost! The possibility of change was blocked by a repression that itself depended on informers. The paradox is that there was so much inventiveness and productivity waiting to be unleashed, so much joy that asked only to be able to express itself. And there was an awareness of the rapidity of social transformation, which showed extraordinary foresight. In no other European country was this anticipation clearer than Italy. When Schumpeter spoke of the real innovation represented by the latest phase of capitalist development, he meant exactly this: an experiment whereby capitalism would be diffused throughout society as a whole. Take a recent development in production such as computerization: it is not computerization that brought about the socialization of production; it was the socialization of production that made computerization necessary. And this led to something new—the socialization of capital. Businessmen didn't want to see this in the 1970s, but they wound up accepting it ten years later—

Along with the loss of ideals!

The repression quite obviously corrupted something—one doesn't massacre a generation without leaving traces. And the political and social management of this transformation was retarded as a result. The transition from material to immaterial production is something that the Communist party and the unions didn't succeed in bringing about. A whole series of styles of life was born—because the transition was ontological, profound: people modified the rhythm of their lives, their social and personal relationships. In reality, they discovered that this new form of labor was more meaningful, that it disrupted the existing balance of power—and gave rise to other power relations. This is exactly what we were saying, thirty years ago.

That workers had entered into postmodernity?

Yes, but it must be understood that this postmodernity, this Italian Silicon Valley that is found today in the northeast of the country, was made by people who came from extreme poverty and the experience of internal immigration, and that it was political struggle that enabled them to change their conditions of life. This is an old Marxist idea, that struggles are what make history; not only history, in fact, because such struggles diffuse a certain consciousness everywhere. This is one way of expressing a principle that is found in all my theoretical work.

In other words, action nonetheless assumes the appearance of a struggle.

Yes, because action is a struggle to constitute the world, to invent it. I am convinced that great progress has already been made in transforming nature, in going beyond it. To act, to struggle, means to create.

It is not nature in and of itself that is the principal enemy, then.

Absolutely not—nature is a friend, even if it is sometimes synonymous with famine or cold. I have horrible memories of the cold: childhood memories during the war, adult memories associated with prison. It was terrible how prison repeated my childhood experience.

Did it bring back memories of the terrible poverty you knew as a child?

Yes—but as a child I always had my mother to see me through it all! The maternal figure on the one hand, and the community of friends on the other: the wealth of affective relationships provides a warmth that is enormously helpful. My mother died while I was in prison. I wasn't allowed to leave to see her before she died, not even once. Nor was I permitted to attend her funeral. Italy is a Catholic country, and therefore a cruel country. And a hypocritical one. They tell you that your mother is dead in a quavering voice—but forget about being let out even for a half-day: prison is not only about being shut away from society; it is also about suffering. If one doesn't suffer, one doesn't atone for one's crime. I remember that I had terrible rheumatic pains afterward. My whole body reacted, remembered. That was in 1982.

Those years must have been very hard.

The situation was completely crazy—there was enormous violence. And yet I continued to think, to write, to work. You can't imagine what the protest movement represented in the 1970s. There was joy.

Joy operates by means of a mechanism of experience, a process, a way in which the relation between the world and one-self can always be changed. There is no such thing as solitary joy. Solitary joy is the joy of saints, but in Milan the people weren't saints—they only experienced the world together. There was total immanence: it was an experience made, lived, wished for. The sharing of this experience is liberty. All this is what the Greeks called *bios*, which is to say life in its entirety. Wages are

not more important than struggle, nor the family more important than the community, nor intellectual life more important
than the care of the body: the absolutely revolutionary thing was
just this—to want to live the totality of human experience. In
this relation between action and *bios* there was an expectation of
transformation, a whole idea of the future. Too often one forgets
that thought requires time to develop. The Italian situation, and
its exceptional duration, permitted these experiences as well as
the formulation of a genuinely revolutionary mode of thinking.
What the French call "*pensée 68*" didn't really occur in France—
it was too brief. There are only one or two thinkers of the period
who continue today to think through this event and its consequences, both real and symbolic. In Germany intellectual ascen-
dancy very quickly passed to followers of the Frankfurt School.
But in Italy there were at least two or three very important cur-
rents of thought and experience, at once negative and positive:
on the one hand, the phenomenon of the Red Brigades and
small terrorist groups, and, on the other, intellectuals and workers, students and women, each with their own other affilia-
tions—what was called the "movement."

*Would you have been imprisoned if there hadn't been a new mode
of thinking?*

Truly revolutionary thought is a very dangerous thing. Look at
the reaction of *L'Osservatore Romano*, the official Vatican daily,
to news of the pardon recently granted one of the *brigatisti*: "It
must not be forgotten that the last few years have seen a kind of
ex cathedra return of the ideological principles of terrorism, of

figures such as Toni Negri and Renato Curcio.[6] Not only do they enjoy a regime of more or less restricted freedom, but they are once again actors on the social scene." This is a veritable inquisition! Twenty years later you are allowed only the right of being invisible. You are forever guilty, in perpetuity.

As if you had encouraged people to commit crimes—

That isn't the question. Curcio, the founder of the Red Brigades, served thirty years in prison. He has paid—why keep on hounding him?

You say that thought requires time.

Yes, it takes time for the thought of a period to develop. There is no 1968 "label," no evidence of *origine controlée* that supports a claim to absolute authenticity. And yet 1968 has become an easily manipulated logo. I am one of those who think that 1968 brought about a new relationship between action and life that implies a fundamental and long-term change of paradigm, one that modified the relationship to life, to history. Nineteen sixty-eight was not a revolution—it was the reinvention of the production of life.

From that point on life has been experienced in a different

---

6. Renato Curcio, one of the founders of the Red Brigades, was arrested in 1975 and sentenced to thirty years in prison. In the late 1990s he was released on parole.

way. Even capitalism has become different, with the virtualization of work and the globalization—the socialization—of production, the progressive disappearance of nation-states. Lived experience has become completely different: the intellectual is no longer a figure who can be separated from life, from the passions. It is always said that the great revolution of thought occurred with Marx, with Freud, but this is utterly ridiculous. The real change has come about through the reconquest of life that has occurred since then. Domination and power are clever: they reigned over life because they understood that it had to be divided up—into work, emotions, the public, the private—in order to be conquered. And the modern idea of the state has operated for centuries in the same way, through division and fear. From this point of view, the recomposition of life was fundamental: one of the slogans of the 1970s was "We want it all." This is what is important: everything.

As a child you knew poverty. . . .

I was born in the Veneto, in Padua. My family had settled there in the 1930s. I remember it when it was an extremely poor region, when people were obliged every year to look for work elsewhere as seasonal laborers. But they didn't leave with their families, they set off alone. This was a very Catholic region. The great axis of emigration for its people was Switzerland, Germany, France, and Belgium. Today the Veneto is perhaps the richest area in all of Europe. The change that has taken place there in forty years is incredible. A region that once was scarcely richer than Sicily is today the most prosperous in Italy, with 7.8

million inhabitants! I remember the war years in the country-side. Like the peasants we lived in extreme poverty, and thanks to them we survived because they gave us what they had—it was a shared poverty. Our house was moldy and damp up to your eyes, the roofs were poorly insulated. It rained inside. There was no hot water. My father was town hall secretary in a small town near Modena and one of the founders of the Italian Communist party at Livorno in 1921. During the fascist period he was humiliated, beaten, hounded. They wound up kicking him out. He died in 1936. I was two years old. My mother was a primary school teacher. She began to work when my father died. She left at five in the morning and came back in the evening: she had three children to feed. My mother helped us in every way she could—she worked like mad so that we could survive.

My father was a worker, from a proletarian family in Bologna. He went to college, taking courses at night. My mother came from a family of small landowners in Mantua, very gener-ous people who did everything they could for her—but they didn't have much, sometimes a little butter or cheese to spare. Today, the transformation of the Veneto is incredible. I'm happy that its people have become rich, but the change has been unimaginably rapid. It is difficult today to describe what it was like there until the early 1960s. I remember one day—I was a junior secretary of the Socialist Federation of Padua—I being told: "Listen, there's a demonstration being planned in a village because the priest is going to prevent Fellini's *La Dolce Vita* from being shown. Something has to be done." I decided to go there to see for myself what was going on. I found that the people were protesting against this priest, who was a real dictator. This was a time when women at the factory didn't have the right to wear pants even though it was very dangerous to work in a skirt. I will always remember the projector grinding away and a crowd of 10,000 people watching *La Dolce Vita* outside, in the dark of night, because the mayor, a Christian Democrat who supported the priest, had cut off the electricity in this part of the village— Fellini in the land of neorealism! It was incredible. It was inside these deep contradictions, on the basis of them, that everything began.

Let's continue: A as in Assassination Attempt—

I never made an attempt on anyone's life—I was accused of having committed hold-ups.

Hold-ups?

Yes, going into a bank and taking money. But I did not take part in any assassination attempt—I find that vile. Stealing money, if it's necessary, I can understand: it is an act. As Brecht said, it's hard to say which is the greater crime: founding a bank or robbing it. Let's use the word "action" instead. In an action there is both a looking forward to the future and the future itself— which is not true for an attempt on someone's life, because this is another morality. I believe I might just barely be able to understand it; but not to share the motivation for it.

Let's talk about A as in Action then.

To act is to form our domain, if we consider philosophy as something that helps us to live. There is an essential relation between thought and action: what the Germans call *Erlebnis*, or lived experience—reflection about experience, experience for reflection; or, if you like, reflection for life, experienced and reflected upon both, which leads on to action.

The sole criterion of truth, for me, is action, which is to say what makes it possible to arrive at the truth. Truth is itself an action—a linguistic acting, a verification, a confrontation. When one acts one goes beyond solitude because to act is to search for the truth, and truth is always experienced in common. One escapes from solitary experience only in action. Action is not a muscular movement or a physical effort, but the search for the common. I imagine that my lifelong fondness for this type of argument is due to the education that I received. I had a socialist-communist education. I have been an activist, and for me there is no truth outside the common—outside what can belong to everyone and what can be verified in language, in cooperation, and in work. A truth is a collective action on the part of persons who campaign together and who transform themselves. I see action as something that constitutes the community, that produces the substance of our dignity and our life. The meaning of action is posited at this level. At several points in the course of my sentimental, philosophical, and political education I found myself rediscovering community: at Padua, for example, at the very beginning of the 1960s, when I was finishing my undergraduate studies and two new lives suddenly opened up to me at the same time: as a researcher and as a political activist. We all felt frustrated by the society in which we were living, and we discovered another way of living in community. We studied and worked together—there were many of us who did this. It seemed to us that we incarnated a modern version of the Averroism found in Padua in the sixteenth century, a great materialist and atheist school; that we were in the service of a *general intellect* that comprehends action, exactly as in Spinoza. And action is precisely the search for and the construction of the common, which is also to say the affirmation of its absolute immanence. But for us, action was also the *passion* of the common. What I am most afraid of, really, is lacking passion.

Reading is a passion as well. My eldest daughter used to say to me: you've given me nothing to read, though you yourself have read tens of thousands of books! Yet as a filmmaker she has a visual talent that I envy. To be able to understand and transform the world in images is an art.

Today life has changed and, contrary to what is believed, people have become more communist than before. In my generation we were trained to do things all alone. Today levels of community and sharing exist everywhere: even writing an article on a computer means having to rely on a common knowledge, which is to say the Internet. Language has now become the most advanced form of community: one no longer exists outside of language. And when this language becomes visual, the body itself interprets the common. Bodily knowledge is a combination of knowledge, passions, visions, behaviors, desires, reappropriations—an indestructible combination.

I must come back for a moment to the concept of *bios*, however, because I believe that it represents a very important extension of the concept of action. The crisis of the 1970s, the duration of this crisis, its depth—these things made up the revolutionary movement, action become *bios*. In Italy it involved a general movement that opposed the marketing of society and prefigured new styles of life. We are witnessing the emergence of a movement of resistance on the part of all minority cultures against the marketing of the world. To act is at once a form of knowledge and a revolt.

This movement therefore has a variety of sources. Its roots in the working class are fundamental: workers had reached the limit of what they could put up with in the context of the Taylorist organization of labor. The communists had directly linked the possibility of resistance to this class of mass-workers. Once again, the communist tradition is rooted in resistance. But the problem was that, once this level of crisis had been reached, the old schema no longer sufficed. "Refuse to work" became the workers' watchword. From the early 1960s I had worked on the experimental journal *Quaderni Rossi*, which gave birth to what would later be called "Italian operaism."[7] I therefore saw the birth of this movement of rejection at the Fiat plant in Turin and at Porto Marghera, the industrial and chemical complex near Venice—the *Petrolchimico*. Even so, I absolutely did not expect to see this rejection explode with the violence and force that it

---

7. *Operaismo* (workerism) grew out of studies of capitalist development and Italian society published by a group of young scholars (notably Panzieri, Tronti, Alquati, Asor Rosa, and Negri) in *Quaderni Rossi* between 1959 and 1962. The operaist theory of workers' struggles, based on a coordinated analysis of institutions, parties, and the history of socialism, was subsequently elaborated in journals such as *Classe Operaia*, *Contropiano*, and *Potere Operaio*.

did after 1968. The "movement" drew strength as well from a second impetus, one that arose from the crisis of the Catholic world and that led to the election of Pope John XXIII. For the first time the Catholic faithful began to struggle in the factories alongside the Communists. This is why 1968 lasted ten years in Italy and why the revolt became deepened, through its capacity for reform, through its practices of "autoreduction" and reappropriation, the institution of "liberated" and self-managed neighborhoods, the invention of a new activism and a new form of political action.

Joy is a way of linking us to the world—it is inseparable from the common, from immanent life. All this I call *bios*: the anticipation of transformation and the concept of the future. Thought requires time. Developing a conception of the future requires time. Nineteen sixty-eight will never be repeated, but it is nonetheless an irreversible event; nothing will ever again be as it once was. In the last thirty years the concept of lived experience has radically changed: henceforth the intellectual can no longer be separated from the life of the passions; the different parts of man have once again been united. We have in our hands the promise of a fearless society. This is what Spinoza said—and what has been rediscovered by feminists, workers, students, and all those who hoped and wished that something would change in 1968, four centuries after Spinoza. Something has changed: life has been reassembled in a new way.

(continued from page 2) others. An anarchist named Giusseppe Pinelli was immediately arrested. Three days later Pinelli died during the course of interrogation, as a result of falling from a fifth-floor window. Subsequent investigation failed to show the least connection between the Piazza Fontana attack and anarchist circles. In the years that followed the extreme Left—and especially *Lotta Continua*, the group's eponymous newspaper—repeatedly denounced the handling of the case, explicitly challenging the police superintendent who conducted the interrogation, Luigi Calabresi, often in very threatening terms. In 1972 a three-man commando squad assassinated Calabresi. A subsequent inquiry ascribed responsibility for the Piazza Fontana attack to the extreme Right and to "rogue secret services." In the meantime, in the mid-1970s, Lotta Continua was dissolved. In 1986, a former member of Lotta Continua named Leonardo Marino told the police, under circumstances that remain still very unclear today, that Calabresi's assassination had been ordered by Sofri and carried out by two other members of the group, Ovidio Bompressi and Giorgio Pietrostefani. A judicial soap opera ensued. The trial was reviewed several times and finally annulled by the Court of Appeals. Purported evidence disappeared or evaporated in the course of preliminary investigation of the case. Contradictory testimony failed to be taken into account. (The historian Carlo Ginzburg compared the conduct of the trial to a witch hunt.) After all this, Sofri, Bompressi, and Pietrostefani were each sentenced to twenty-two years in prison for the assassination of Calabresi. They began serving their terms in February 1997, twenty-five years after the superintendant's death. By virtue of the law that absolves "penitents" of guilt, their accuser, Marino, was freed. The three who had been accused protested their innocence. Pietrostefani, taking advantage of a temporary grant of liberty, fled during the final review of the case; Sofri and Bompressi chose to remain to testify against the miscarriage of justice to which they had been subjected. Bompressi's sentence was later suspended on grounds of ill health, since incarceration would have endangered his life. Sofri, despite a great many calls for his release, is still in prison today, in Pisa. He continues to proclaim his innocence, having gone so far as to refuse a pardon—since this is granted only to those who are guilty. The authors of the attack in the Piazza Fontana have never been arrested.

In the 1970s a series of anonymous attacks—notably in the Piazza della Loggia in Brescia in May 1974 (where the explosion of a bomb at a labor protest killed eight and wounded 103), and the bombing of the train *Italicus* the following August (killing twelve and wounding forty-four)—inaugurated what was called the "strategy of tension." Each new attack increased suspicions of collusion between groups on the extreme Right and certain fringe elements of the intelligence services. In the early 1990s a new series of bloody attacks in Rome, Florence, and Milan reinforced this impression and raised the possibility of a still more disturbing link between "rogue services" and the Mafia.

B AS IN . . .

B as in Brigate Rosse.

One must be careful not to think of the Red Brigades as making up the whole of the movement of the 1970s, and of this movement as a historical parenthesis, an absolutely isolated, singular, separate term; in reality, the movement was a path in life, one taken by a great many of my generation. There are many people—sometimes ingenuous, more often stupid—who continue to portray me as the head of the Red Brigades, the malign mastermind. To be a professor and to be active in politics or, if you prefer, an academic and a communist could only mean one thing—a *cattivo maestro*, a wicked teacher. . . .

Why did all this happen so differently in Italy?

Following the publication of *Empire*, the book I wrote with the American philosopher Michael Hardt, several American journalists asked me why Italy was the only country that had never come to terms with the events of May 1968. What has happened is absurd. I could show you people who today hold positions of power in Europe and who shared the same experiences as I did—they're not in prison! Everything is turned around. It isn't my story in particular that is interesting—it's the story of a generation that needs to be told in order to explain why such a state of affairs exists in 2001: some are still in exile or in prison while others have become powerful men.

It needs to be kept in mind that Italy is a Catholic country. In the mid-1970s, and in response to 1968, there was a perverse alliance between Catholicism and Stalinism. What was called the "historic compromise" was an agreement between the Communist party and the Christian Democrats to conduct a common policy. Through this alliance the communists were detached from the revolutionary ideal, which is to say the representation of the poor and the workers: the great Italian repression was felt by all those who denounced this. For after 1968, in Italy as elsewhere, there was an enormous hope for change that was sustained by struggles—in the factories, in the universities, in women's groups—and it was this hope that the historic compromise crushed. Only repression remained then. Moreover, the entire left-wing European intelligentsia supported the Italian Communist party (PCI) because it enjoyed a certain independence vis-à-vis the USSR. But in reality the PCI paid for this freedom by allying itself with the government in ways that involved death, betrayal, espionage, provocations.

Demonstrations were organized at the time in Italy, calling the people to take up arms.

Yes, we have already mentioned this. In Italy, between 1943 and 1945, there was an extremely powerful war of resistance. Twenty-five years later, in 1968, the memory was still alive, because antifascism had been linked to the class struggle. The poor in Italy, at least in the north, remained antifascist. By the 1960s the extraparliamentary Left had penetrated all social classes, particularly in the factories. The break with the official Communist party occurred at that level, which was very harmful to the party—precisely because the opposition to it came from the workers. It's hard to imagine such a thing happening today. Moreover, since the PCI was particularly open to Western values and inclined to take issue with the Soviet line, repressing the extreme Left meant entering straight away into the official system of the parties of the "free world." At this point people reacted. Imagine what would have happened if, in France, there had been an extreme Left majority at Renault or Citroën. In France, during the events of May 1968, it was the intellectuals who led the movement of revolt, not the workers. In Italy the opposite occurred: the workers who rejected the historic compromise led the struggles, not the intellectuals.

The members of the Red Brigades with whom I was in prison during the 1980s and after my return, in 1997, came from working-class backgrounds. They really believed they could bring about a revolution.

They didn't think that a peaceful solution was possible?

No one thought so at the time, myself included. Still today I believe that state-sponsored violence exists; and that the response can be nonviolent, though surely not peaceful—in any case, nonviolent resistance is still resistance. Capitalism itself isn't peaceful! It cannot survive without violence. We are told that capitalism is natural, because the market and exchange are the natural forms of civil life: we are led to believe that there is no other way to create forms of production and reproduce wealth and life. And so? Surely all this is violence. The problem at the time wasn't the search for a peaceful solution. It was to choose between resistance to this armed violence, as I did, and the use of this very violence, as the Red Brigades did.

In Italy, in order to conquer terrorism, the government and the police proceeded to mount two operations: the criminalization of intellectuals who took part in the struggles; and the encouragement of informers. The system of relying on "penitents" [*pentiti*], which is to say the legal recognition of denunciation, gave freedom to all persons who were willing to confess, no matter what charges had been brought against them. Some had committed a dozen assassinations and were freed immediately! Many of them told the authorities whatever they wanted to hear in order to get out. Those who thought in a certain way were criminalized, and the others were used to accuse them. And so when a militant was arrested, weapon in hand, the police said to him: "You can either languish in prison and risk your neck, my friend, or you can talk. . . ." Some told the truth, which was tragic in and of itself since it led to dozens of arrests; others told lies and sent innocent people to jail. As I say, most of those charged in my trial, the Sette Aprile trial, were acquitted after six or seven years in prison. Still today the same method is employed: the police take action only in a fraction of cases, because these involve exemplary offenses—ones that correspond to certain statistical patterns and need to be made examples of. The main job of the police in this connection is to find inform-ers. All those who think of the police exclusively as a "public body," as a physical force devoted to the protection of citizens, make a great error. The other police, the immaterial police, is the one that creates order on the basis of denunciation, with all the consequences that you may imagine follow from this.

C AS IN . . .

C as in Camp.

In Italian, unlike French, the same word [*campo*] is used to express the concepts of "camp" and "field." I naturally think, then, of choosing my camp as a farmer goes to work his field, or as a linguist explores semantic fields. French is a complex language. In French, I should also choose my camp in the sense of finding oneself on a field of battle—but it is precisely this logic that I reject, and that I search for a way out from. To choose one's camp, all right—so long as one does this in order to cultivate the field and to make things grow in it: plants, desires, bonds. Life, in other words. Not war.

The real problem in any case is choosing one's own camp, choosing a kind of political activism. There is no truth that does not derive from choosing sides, because truth is never neutral. To claim that science is neutral condemns it to powerlessness. Political militancy is the form through which the joy of truth and the pleasure of life are rendered accessible. Militancy develops a linguistic field that corresponds to the fullness of passions; militancy transforms the flesh of life into a singular body. I understood this when I was young: choosing a camp amounted to choosing a destiny. But it was also a choice of poverty—choosing to remain with others, those who were the most impoverished, the most excluded. On the one hand there was the choice of engagement; on the other, the human condition of the most desperate. When I think of the role played in contemporary philosophy by what is called "negative thought" (from Nietzsche to Benjamin and from Rosenzweig to Agamben), I am reminded that these thinkers perceived the existence of a limit, a boundary, where the force of living is liberated—even if they did so in a disembodied way. My only reservation in this regard is that this limit can't correspond to a "behind us," located in an indeterminate history and an indeterminate space. It is in front of us—it is the edge of time, the instant, the point at which each of our vital projections shoots off into the void. This is what choosing one's camp means to me: to be engaged and, at the same time, to rediscover the naked condition of life. And also: to treat each moment as innovation of life, in a time that is creation.

D AS IN . . .

D as in Defeat.

There have been two real wounds in my life: one due to departure, the other to return. My departure from Italy amounted to a recognition of defeat—a decision that, under the circumstances, I had to leave in order to stay alive, not only physically (for indeed there were threats against my life), but above all intellectually. Life was important to me, and the first thing I did on arriving in exile in Paris was to have a child. My youngest daughter was born in 1984 and is now seventeen years old. For me and for her mother, who was my companion at the time, it was a way of reaffirming life.

The second wound was opened by my return to Italy—I bring it up again now because it's a complex thing. I wanted to go back because it seemed possible politically, twenty years later, to pick up the pieces. I discussed the idea with friends in Paris as well as with a number of Italian politicians, all of whom seemed to agree it made sense. But when I got there everything fell apart. No sooner had I arrived in Italy than I was accused of having selfishly come back to settle a personal problem—my prison sentence. The judges assigned to my case gave me another three and a half years! I experienced all this as a real betrayal, a disaster—as if one wanted to rewrite history. Fortunately friends were there to help—

Friends who had remained in Italy?

Yes—and among them I found a community. I began to work and to reinvent things. I haven't fathered another child, but that will happen one day!

Today, when you think of the wound caused by your flight to France, do you have any regrets?

I left because the political struggle, such as we had envisaged it, was finished. A period of our individual and collective life, a certain historical singularity, had come to an end. Later I wrote an article whose themes I have reworked several times since, because it well describes the kind of awareness and doubt we shared at that moment. The article is entitled "In Praise of the Absence of Memory."

Why "absence of memory"?

Because memory determines continuity. And continuity is always the expression of power. It was necessary to sustain a subjective point of view, to combat the "blurring" of history by which the authorities sought to mask our role and to create an appearance of continuity. It is this blurring of reality that pushed us off course, and that continues still today to hold us back.

And that prevented the revolt from succeeding?

It didn't stop the revolt—it swallowed the revolt whole. It destroyed everything that led toward revolt. Revolt is never only a matter of action. Revolt, the forces of opposition, grow out of resistance, reflection. The combination of these new powers becomes very important: it determines the content of struggles. By the beginning of the 1980s struggle had become impossible. Carrying on with the revolt, which had been our aim, no longer had any meaning, neither from the point of view of the subject—because the working class and all the other participants in the struggle were in the process of changing—nor from the point of view of critical consciousness. All that had to be reinterpreted. For me, this search for a new purpose was absolutely fundamental. I detest people who say, "The working class is dead and the struggle goes on." No: if the working class is dead—which is true—then the whole system linked to this relation of forces is thrown into crisis. The victory of the authorities in the late 1970s did not reaffirm the old system but, on the contrary, profoundly modified it, making possible new forms of resistance and struggles, new lines of flight. It was therefore necessary to adapt to this new situation, to respond to trends, to the reality of the new relations of power that this transformation implied. This was a moment, then, of great historical changes: the transition from Fordism to post-Fordism, from the modern to the postmodern. These changes transformed not only the structures of production and power, but also personal feelings, forms of language, and expressions of desire. And so this is what happened. New codes were established, new forms of command were imposed, new controls were put into place—tearing apart the whole system. From a subjective point of view the weight of this change, its enormity, seemed unbearable. The old form of life and struggle was now shattered in a thousand pieces: as if each positive response devised by practical action and critical thought had now been ruled out once and for all. Life became more complicated by the day, and the obstacles higher and more difficult to overcome.

You therefore left Italy at a crucial moment, when your survival was at stake.

I fell into a terrible depression. That begins with D, doesn't it?

Was it a matter of being profoundly discouraged or a genuine case of depression? Weren't you nonetheless excited to be in another country?

No—France was a country that I knew well, there wasn't even the attraction of novelty. Mitterrand had won but this was already 1983, in September. It was a period of relative crisis, of changes. The euphoria of 1981 had evaporated. A sense of disillusionment with Mitterrandism was already being felt. I was in an extremely serious situation. I had abandoned my friends in Italy. The entire Italian press was outraged by my flight, which it treated as an act of betrayal. The idea that one cannot flee is particularly strong in Italy: to flee is to betray. It was obvious that the Right was going to treat me as a coward. What is incredible is that the Left dragged me through the mud. The Left said, "We had confidence in him, we elected him deputy, we elected him to represent us in our struggles against the emergency laws about social protest and terrorism, and he has left. He has abandoned us." The Communist party hated me because I was the symbol and the reflection of its own crisis, and because it was obliged to learn the lessons of this crisis. And the extreme Left—or at least what was left of it—wound up taking a completely unrealistic position, no doubt because it was still convinced that it could win, which was crazy. It hadn't admitted defeat. Myself, I had finally understood, even if from the psychological point of view it remained very difficult to accept.

You had the feeling that you had really abandoned your friends?

No—but, you know, it wasn't easy. It was as if I were going away forever. Great political events are not the only things that are hard to live through. There are also all the simpler things, where one often has the impression of being in the right—it always takes time to realize how much others have suffered. In particular there were prison comrades with whom I had very intense, very strong relationships.

And they don't feel betrayed?

They do—not all of them, but a good many. And given the situation in which we found ourselves, those who didn't feel betrayed couldn't really say so, if only because for the guards, for the police, that would have represented a sort of exaltation of my flight. They faced a heavy sentence, the trials were under way or pending—it wasn't a joking matter. The most opportunistic among them said: "We are not like Negri—we stayed here. Negri betrayed us." The others, those who agreed with me, said nothing. The Right and the Left attacked me. I was said to be a bad philosopher, a *cattivo maestro*, a wicked teacher, because my behavior wasn't Socratic: one must accept the law even if the law is unjust, because that is the only way to defend oneself. But you've still got to be able to defend yourself! I was given thirty years in prison on the basis of wild denunciations made by "penitents." I had only just left, having waited more than four years for a trial that never came. Once I was no longer there the trial could begin. All that was needed were a few people willing to accuse me of anything and everything: they wanted to get out of prison, I was on the run—no defense was possible.

In France, did you have immediate access to the means to survive, not only materially but also psychologically, and to continue to write?

I had many friends. There was Félix Guattari, my dearest friend. For a long time my name was Guattari because Félix found me a place to live. My first apartment had been furnished by Amnesty

International. It was on the Place d'Italie, on the nineteenth or twentieth floor. I was shut up inside there for two or three months. I remember watching the birds whirl about in the air and then suddenly swoop and dive. I also remember looking down at the cars, which seemed tiny from such a height—and then again at the birds, the cars. . . .

So I fathered a child. It was the only thing to do. A splendid little girl. That was a terrific idea. We didn't know what to do— so we did the only reasonable thing. At bottom it was very amusing. Amusing and terrible at the same time, because we were starting over again from nothing. In Italy the hatred for what I symbolized had stabilized, almost solidified. The president of the republic had made a speech saying that I was the vilest type of person that could be imagined, an example of the worst Lombrosian type,[8] a psychopathic criminal, loathsome, dangerous. When it is the president of the republic who says this, it isn't really very funny. It was an incredible act of violence, the worst part of which was that there were honest and intelligent people ready to believe it.

And so the idea became fixed in people's minds.

Yes. I live with that still, today. One has the impression there's more tolerance now, because I'm locked away in prison. But it doesn't take much for the cycle to start up again: an article, par-

---

8. The reference is to the work of the Italian physician Cesare Lombroso (1835–1909), one of the founders of modern criminology, who developed the theory of the "born criminal."—Trans.

ticipation in a conference, a book that does well in the United States. When it isn't resentment, it's envy.

When did Félix Guattari enter your life?

In fact I knew Deleuze before Guattari. I met Félix in 1978, and we continued to correspond regularly while I was incarcerated. He came down to see me, in prison, and he arranged for me to come to France. He found lawyers, he prepared my exile. He rented an apartment for me in his brother's name. It was a very beautiful apartment looking out upon a courtyard.

Did he really had this charisma that everyone talks about so much, more so than Deleuze?

Deleuze was a delightful character, but he was a professor, an intellectual! We talked about many things, but I couldn't tell him that I was depressed, that I was tired, that I had problems. I couldn't ask him to do anything for me. It was difficult to explain to him what was happening in Italy. With Félix I could. Very soon we began to come up with ideas together—and not only from the theoretical point of view. With the help of the German Greens we formed the first such organization in France. Félix was a friend of Danny Cohn-Bendit, but especially with his brother. I had a friend who was a leading political figure in Germany, a member of the Green party that came out of 1968. With their help we organized a meeting under the auspices of the Protestant Church in Paris that brought together the whole French extreme Left, from Yves Cochet to Krivine.

The purpose of these meetings, which lasted from 1984 to 1986, was to try to create a union between the Reds and the Greens. Félix was attuned to intellectual life in Paris—he followed cultural developments, everything experimental. And he had a small coterie, many of them very intelligent, interesting people, although by the time I arrived in France they played less of a role than before. Félix had an incredible ability to listen. He knew everyone, which gave me the opportunity to meet all the important figures of the current scene, everyone we thought was interesting. It was great.

And did the Reds and the Greens enter into an alliance?

No, because the Trotskyites were unwilling to participate. In France, the Greens had actually been invented by Mitterrand—they weren't a truly autonomous political construction. The system of proportional representation allowed both the *lepéniste* extreme Right and the Greens to appear. The Greens later became something else; but at the time it was difficult. We hadn't succeeded in giving concrete form to our plans. On the one hand there were the Trotskyites, and on the other there was the crisis of the Left, which found itself in disarray. The only possibility of moving forward was through the great march on behalf of the *beurs*.[9] Nonetheless there was this one new thing—it was inter-

---

9. Negri is referring here to the March for Equality that took place in Paris on December 1, 1984 to show solidarity with the cause of second-generation Arab immigrants (known by the French slang term *beurs*) in the face of growing support for the National Front.—Trans.

esting. It was the beginning of the movement for the rights of the *beurs*: a new hybridization.

With SOS Racisme, among others.[10]

I began to write a few short articles about things of this nature. On this strange white, black, green, yellow Orpheus—this new group of people that one was starting to find everywhere in 1986 and 1987. The idea of hybridization was necessary since it expanded horizons again. For a long time we'd lived off of the theme of the "local" becoming "global": *glocal*, as the Americans called it. Today people speak several languages and have several levels of language. And it isn't a question only of children of immigrants but of our own children, because our culture is now entirely mixed. I think this is fantastic—there's a total freedom of mixing and hybridizing, which makes it possible to express new feelings, different emotions. And this in turn constructs new subjects, subjects having neither boundaries nor fixed identities.

Awareness of this process did in fact begin with the beur *movement, which provoked a very violent reaction on the part of the National Front.*

---

10. SOS Racisme, an antiracist movement with chapters throughout France and in Switzerland, was founded in 1984 by student activists from the Union des Étudiants Juifs de France (UEJF) and organizers of the March for Equality. In recent years it has come under attack by politicians on both the Right and the Left.—Trans.

And this is a phenomenon that, in France, in large part antici-pated what subsequently happened in the other major European countries. As always, a brief digression is in order: the problem of anticipations. If there is a minor sort of scientific talent that I can take pride in, it is that I have almost always managed to understand in advance what is going to happen next. This "ten-dential" method, as it used to be called, consists in anticipating the value of things that form an evolving system of tendencies, or trends, which is to say things one thinks will end up coming to pass in the future.

What is this method based on?

The first thing we noticed were changes in the domain of labor. Certain transformations of labor immediately manifested them-selves, both in everyday life and in the life of cities, in the way in which people lived. The new organization of labor did in fact anticipate new forms of life. Today the problem has become still more profound, because forms of life are now organized on the basis of production. In other words, the forms of life themselves are used to generate profit. I say "forms of life" because I am speaking also of language, which is to say the very possibility of communicating. We are therefore faced with two aspects of one and the same tendential transformation: on the one hand, the increasingly immaterial and communicative nature of labor, and on the other, the hybridization of forms, which is to say of their biopolitical content.

When I left Italy, I was constantly aware of this change. I felt sure that a real rupture had taken place, a true change of paradigm: another world was in the process of being formed, and we knew it. Was it a question of passing from the modern to the postmodern? The postmodern began as a literary category, but it rapidly became something ontological, profoundly linked to all these ways in which people lived, these ways of producing and reproducing. A new and comprehensive perception of the body, a new perception of the power of life.

Apart from Guattari, whom did you feel close to when you were in Paris? Were you warmly received in psychoanalytic circles?

I was still trying to make sense of this rupture, this passage from one world to another. I had Félix as a friend and Deleuze as a fellow philosopher. And, along with Deleuze, a group of Spinozists who were really great friends: Alexandre Matheron, Pierre-François Moreau, Étienne Balibar, and others. And then there were the Marxists in crisis: Jean-Marie Vincent, Denis Berger, people who had struggled, constructed systems—the whole Paris-VIII group that had left Vincennes for Saint-Denis. Also exiled Italians, many of them very intelligent, very politicized people, almost all of whom had become university professors, restaurateurs, executives, and so on—in short, geniuses of resourcefulness. There are still 150 of them who can't go back to Italy: twenty years have passed, they have created another life for themselves, they now have white hair, and many of them live well. The fact remains that they have suffered a grave injury.

Were you the only one who believed that you could come back without creating a fuss?

Yes. I was really a fool—but I was also the only one who could afford to be a fool.

Had you been warned?

Yes, but I wasn't in a position to understand—I was having personal problems as well. I was in the process of separating from the woman who was my companion at the time, which I experienced as a betrayal, a private wound in addition to the wound of my departure. This separation coincided exactly with my return to Italy. With the benefit of hindsight, I believe I can see the matter more clearly. Was it the separation that made me want to go back or did my desire to return cause the separation? It was more the latter, I think. My former companion remained in France and has since married and had two children. I am happy for her, but at the time it was difficult for me to accept. I have had to confront many different and complex affective situations in my life, but I believe that in this case the same drama that occurred when I left Italy played itself out again, only in reverse. There was a genuine betrayal of the pact of confidence and solidarity that we had entered into. The betrayal represented by this separation was similar to what I had experienced on leaving Italy, by abandoning the others—now it was the other way around. I had never really managed to work out why I had such a strong desire to leave, despite the terrible anxiety I felt. That took me three months. This was in 1997—I'd finished writing *Empire* with my friend Michael Hardt. We were hoping that my return to Italy would make it possible to pose the problems of the 1970s in fresh terms and to find a political solution for all those who were still in prison or in exile. All this depended on the success of the proposals for constitutional reform that were then being considered in Italy. Everyone was convinced that things were going to work out. But then there was a fierce clash between the Right and the Left, and no further progress could be made. The reform bill failed, the political solution was swallowed up, I remained in prison—and the judges added three and a half years to my sentence, making a total of seventeen and a half. And even though I hope to be able to finish out my term under a regime of "alternative detention,"[11] I will not be completely free until October 2003. Doesn't that seem a bit long?

All these years in prison haven't made you bitter?

I wasn't really accustomed to dealing with institutions in general. Think of the institutions one comes into contact with in the course of one's life. There is school, of course—not always much fun, but this is the way life begins. There's also the army, but this is a very brief experience, not a very happy one, but temporary. And then there is the medical system, which, depending on the country, provides very unequal care, and in any case one would rather not deal with doctors because sickness is frightening— and doctors sometimes make it still more frightening. But for most people that's about it. In the last analysis, no one knows

---

11. Negri's petition for parole was approved, permitting him to serve the balance of his sentence under house arrest from May 2002.—Trans.

what prison is like except those for whom it is a part of life. Prison itself is not terrifying. What is terrifying is, on the one hand, the ignorance and, on the other, the routine.

When you left, did you leave behind your child—the one who was born in Paris?

The little girl? No, she was already in Italy, where she was living with her mother. I saw her during summer vacations. She used to come to France to see me and now she comes to Rome regularly.

In what sense did you feel betrayed when you left France?

The true betrayal was not a matter of being betrayed in love. I don't think of a woman as someone who betrays—that doesn't interest me, at least not the sort of betrayal one finds in light comedies, which would have been both funnier and less serious. In the case of real betrayal, one betrays a whole plan of life, an ethical dimension—not an ideal of fidelity. This wasn't a story of jealousy or possession. I don't understand either of these things.

I think that the feeling of betrayal really exists only if it touches an inner, very primitive chord. Political circumstances by themselves do not give rise to this feeling—it has to be reinforced deep inside us.

Betraying another person, like informing on another person, is related to the fact that there is something singularly transversal among men: this kind of community of love, this transversality of confidences, this construction of language. Betrayal signifies the ruin of an ongoing project of construction. It is, strictly speaking, an act of destruction.

Something intangible?

From the Spinozist point of view, things are fairly clear. What do men represent? Transversalities, combinations of atoms, combination of parts. Now, in all phenomena of rupture, a tissue is torn, whether the tissue is social or political or related to friendship or love. Denunciation and betrayal are examples of this, although one could consider them from various points of view: political denunciation, affective betrayal, denunciation in relation to truth, betrayal of a common project and relation to the body. In the case of denunciation, it is the construction of truth, of intimacy, of genuine complicity that is destroyed, thrown out, ruined. In both cases relations have been constructed that constitute new forms of life; and in both cases their destruction is confirmed. Betrayal and denunciation are, from this point of view, identical: they shatter the "common." In Italy, at the end of the 1970s and the beginning of the 1980s, the crisis and end of the revolutionary movements led to a generalized practice of informing and repenting—denunciation and repentence as instruments of personal and juridical protection imposed by the authorities. A certain number of laws were adopted: talking meant getting out of prison. These are very important laws that still today are used against the Mafia and that have completely changed the character of the Italian legal system. Once again the result is that persons who have assassinated dozens of people are free, while others who have never killed anyone are still in prison. It is a perverse system—its effects are unimaginable.

This system has been the object of criticism for some time now.

No—only with regard to its treatment of commercial offenses.

It is said to have been of great value in the struggle against the Mafia, but this is not clear.

The fact remains, quite apart from any moral judgment about this type of self-interested "repentence," that it is a double-edged sword.

It amounts really to using Mafia methods, doesn't it? Isn't there a temptation to fight one's enemies using their own weapons?

The same practice of denunciation has been used by the Italian courts to attack politicians since the early 1990s, socialists as well as politicians on the Right. It isn't a question of defending this or that political class against the charge of corruption—it is quite obvious they were all unimaginably corrupt; the point is that the courts internalized extremely ambiguous practices and found a new use for them. The Left, as I mentioned earlier, entered the justice system through the struggle against terrorism. It is the Left that led the enterprise of political repression in the late 1970s. Ten years later, using the same instruments, it attacked the socialists and the Christian Democrats—and Berlusconi as well. In a certain sense, we served as guinea pigs.

Which Left are you talking about?

The Communists. The problem is that Berlusconi fought back and won. It's incredible! The idea of corruption has contaminated everything. Even so, one can't simply use the legal system to attack all one's adversaries, one after another! In *Empire* we say exactly this: corruption has become a form of government. Alas, it is not either a defect or a limit—it is a form of government in the full sense of the term. I would like to come back to this point later and develop it further.

Is corruption the only possible condition of nations today?

No—but when you are in a nation where there is no longer any real political representation, only simply more or less adequate forms of advertising and strategies of communication, there is no longer struggle, no longer politics, no longer body.

As in America?

Exactly. Everything happens through spectacle, through television.

And do you find this dangerous or not?

No, I don't find it dangerous—but it isn't inoffensive either. I merely note the fact that it occurs. The question is simply how to use these more or less adequate forms in order to transform them.

Nonetheless there is a future for these forms.

These are the forms in which we live! We don't have the option of doing away with them. Revolution isn't possible in France or Italy. It would be more realistic to propose an alternative power at the world level—to respond to globalization from deep inside its bowels.

E AS IN . . .

E as in Empire. What can you say about the concept of Empire you developed with Michael Hardt?

Our work has been chiefly one of linguistic clarification. In fact, there is a certain lingering ambiguity about the term 'Empire' itself, which entered almost at once into the political and journalistic lexicon and rapidly became static. By 'Empire' we mean something very precise: the transfer of sovereignty of nation-states to a higher entity. But this transfer has almost invariably been interpreted in terms of an "internal analogy"—as if Empire were implicitly a nation-state on a world scale. One consequence of this trivialization has been the rather sloppy inference that Empire corresponds to the United States. We insist, to the contrary, that the great transfers of sovereignty that are now taking place—in the military sphere, in the monetary sphere, and in the cultural, political, and linguistic spheres—cannot be reduced to any such internal analogy. This amounts to saying that the structure of Empire is radically different from that of nation-states.

The process that led to Empire grew out of several contradictory phenomena: the struggles of the working classes in the developed countries against capital, which have rendered the reproduction of the capitalist system impossible on the national scale; the anticolonial wars and Vietnam, which gave rise to very considerable anti-imperialist pressures that left their mark on capital at its highest and most central levels; and, finally, the crisis of the socialist countries, where the socialist management of capital failed to develop in the face of ever greater demands for liberty. Together these things caused imbalances at a global level, with the result that the passage to Empire was punctuated by many extremely violent conflicts. The imperial process that we describe is therefore contradictory both in its origin and its development. Today we have a world *governance* that seeks to impose forms of government that extend to the whole biopolitical tissue of planetary citizenship. What we tried to do in writing this book was to begin to define the fields of struggle and the forces of opposition within the very heart of Empire. This means, above all, establishing fundamental demands that correspond to the new context of economic globalization. I have in mind three demands in particular: the right of circulation, to move about freely as citizens of the world; the right to a social wage, conceived as a minimum "citizenship income"; and the right to reappropriation, which is to say recognition of the fact that production belongs to the many.

First point: the labor force now no longer knows any boundaries. One needs therefore to begin to think in terms of global citizenship. As citizens of the world, people ought to be able to go where they wish; they ought to be able to vote where they are, where they work. Freedom of movement has until now been managed entirely by capital, because it needed low-cost labor and because the mobility of the labor force was essential to the production of value. We demand that this free circulation become a right of the global citizen and that this right formally belong to him.

Second point: a minimum wage. Therefore a system for the distribution of wealth that acknowledges reproduction as something necessary, which is to say both the reproduction of the workforce and the reproduction of humanity. Specifically, this means that to the extent social cooperation and affects are now an integral part of the production of value—think of the function of women in society: as Deleuze used to say, we are witnessing the feminization of labor—we demand that the participation of each person in social capital be remunerated. Which means that everyone must have equal access to health, to knowledge, to material well-being. The world can no longer be torn between rich and poor, between those who are productive and those who are not, because production has become indistinguishable from life itself, so that no division is possible. A guaranteed income, the wage of citizenship, is both the end of the mirage of the politics of assistance and of laws regarding the poor—which serve only to reinforce divisions—and the end of destitution. Since production is entirely biopolitical, it is necessary to remunerate life.

Final point: since life has become the motor of production, we demand that the multitude—which is to say the citizens of the world—be permitted to reappropriate life for themselves. We demand, for example, that there no longer be such a thing as copyright. Why should knowledge, which is today at the center of production, not be accessible to everyone?

Is this the end of the idea of the author?

It is the end of the idea of property. It is difficult to accept the end of the idea of material property; but when it is a question of immaterial property and of immaterial production, this seems simpler. Yet it is the same problem.

This is the whole question posed by the Internet with Napster.

It is not only a question of the Internet. The Internet is simply the part of the iceberg that is the most visible. But almost all production is now carried out this way, through networks of cooperation and exchange. Production cannot be founded on both the circulation of knowledge and the right to limit free access to it. And when I say cooperation, in reality I am saying life. Today, work and life, production and reproduction are entirely mixed together—they feed on one another. In other words, the material wealth of the world arises through forms of collaboration, of cooperation—and not only through intellectual work: contacts, relationships, exchanges, and desires have become productive. Production is life itself. It is by virtue of this fact that everything that lives is part of the system of production. The forms of monetary exchange, the forms of command, the defense of property have, as a consequence, become more parasitic. Thirty years ago one could denounce them in the name of exploitation. Today, changes in the paradigm of production require their elimination. It is a lovely paradox: capitalism has entered into a new phase, and it is capital itself that will fulfill the promises we made in the 1970s and were unable to keep. I speak of failure, but in fact this metamorphosis of capital is precisely the result of our struggles.

And yet at the same time, to take again the example of Napster, progressive forces have lost.

They have lost for the moment, but wait and see what happens in the next few years. . . .

Isn't there always a temptation to put property back at the heart of the debate, even though one senses that the movement goes in the other direction?

Yes. I am not sure this can work for long, however. There was a time when access to the Bible was considered the unchallenge-able prerogative of the Church. Free access to the Bible was considered dangerous by the authorities. Today the problem is posed at the level of knowledge in general, which is to say at the level of language. Language has become the foundation of life. Everything has become linguistic and biopolitical. And the authorities consider as dangerous everything that lies within the reach of the poor, which is to say those who have no other wealth than their life.

Hasn't politics always been biopolitics?

One must be clear about the concept of biopolitics. It literally means the intertwining of power and life. The fact that power has chosen to place its imprint upon life itself, to make life its privileged surface of inscription, is not new: it is what Foucault called "biopower," whose birth at the end of the eighteenth century he described. But resistance to biopower exists. To say that life resists power means that it affirms its own power, which is to say its capacity for creation, invention, production, subjectivation. This is what we call "biopolitical": the resistance of life to power, from within it—inside this power, which has besieged life. From this point of view, the whole history of philosophy is in fact on the side of biopower, with a few exceptions.

E as in Eugenics.

Philosophy almost always exalts eugenics—only the tradition of materialist thought escapes this tendency. I have done a great deal of work on the question of the monster lately, and I promise you that not many monsters are to be found among philosophers! By contrast, one finds an almost constant emphasis on eugenics, up to and including the most recent apologists for power.

Eugenics, as a concept, is the attempt to format life.

Yes—a complete formatting. From this point of view, Nazism is the most extreme example.

From Aristotle to Nazism—you're going a bit too far!

It is not a question of saying that Aristotle was a Nazi, nor of inventing shocking continuities. But there is I believe, something that recurs in a striking way in this connection. One must read Reiner Schürmann, a curious and extremely intelligent Dominican who ended up teaching at the New School for Social Research in New York. Schürmann wrote an exceptional book in which he sought to show the perverse continuity of the theme of eugenics throughout the history of Western metaphysics.[12] Biopolitics, in the sense we give it, is the opposite of eugenics: it is the will to let forms flourish—there is no difference between nature and culture. In reality, all nature is a second, a third, a fourth nature. In other words, hybridization is already and always present. It is this fact that interests us and that must be grasped. But power seized this terrain and made it the foundation for its mechanisms of control. Biodesire must be contrasted with biopower. The desire for life, the strength and wealth of desire, are the only things that we can oppose to power, which needs to place limitations upon biodesire. It is for this reason that power, faced with life, displays two contradictory attitudes: on the one hand, it works to organize life, relating subjects, multitudes, and singularities to each other, linking invention, resistance; and, on the other hand, it imposes control over all this. The whole problem of phi-

---

12. See Reiner Schürmann, *Principe d'anarchie: Heidegger et la question de l'agir* (Paris: Seuil, 1982). An English translation was published by Indiana University Press in 1987 under the title *Heidegger on Being and Acting: From Principles to Anarchy.*—Trans.

losophy, of eugenics, is the identification of the ontological principle—which is to say the principle of organization of Being—with the principle of command and hierarchy imposed on being.

That's rather dangerous.

Yes, but it's not simply dangerous—it's perverse. The problem of philosophical eugenics, which is still with us, is that a certain type of thought that has been dominant for centuries affirms that the principle of Being is also the principle of its control—which was a weird idea from the very beginning. We had to wait for postcolonial and feminist studies in order to situate this original sin! The people of the colonies discovered a world based on the values of imperialist Eurocentrism, in the same way women discovered the principle of patriarchy. In the work of Gayatri Spivak—an Indian philosopher who lives in the United States and who has translated Derrida—the critical synthesis of postcolonialism and feminism gradually begins to define this change in understanding with precision, which makes it possible to clearly formulate the problem of the demystification of eugenics. I find this kind of thing extremely interesting, because it makes it possible to construct an ontological perspective that brings together anticolonialism and feminism, currently the two most important theories of difference. Through the critique of eugenics, these theories work together to construct the common.

Eugenics has never really been much discussed—this recurrent temptation, made possible by technology, to format every aspect of life and of the individual. Is its actual impact something to be feared?

If you are speaking of eugenics in and of itself, I don't know; but all the thematics of hybridization are so many "floating mines" waiting to explode. It is obvious that in the great imperial universities all this is accepted as a matter of course—it is the basis of "political correctness." It is accepted today that blacks and whites can sit next to each other, that a white woman can have a child with a black man, or a black woman with a white man. This had never happened before, the acceptance of this pressure at the highest levels. I was talking about this not so long ago with the Dutch architect Rem Koolhaas, who told me that in his class at Harvard there is an almost total hybridization. This is to say that the ten or fifteen people who study with him include not only the children of the world ruling class (because all corporate leaders send their children there: the whole republican elite, the whole imperial elite is found at Harvard and the other great world universities) but also, because there is a system of scholarships that functions fairly well, the sons and daughters of poor parents. This means that a progressive hybridization now extends beyond the principles of Western political life as these principles have been formulated since the beginning of modernity. Until recently it was supposed that there could be only three forms of government: monarchy, aristocracy, and democracy. But all three were characterized by a fundamental unity and by the rejection of multiplicity, of the multitude and hybridization. For modern political thought, no government is possible without reduction to unity. Hybridization is the difference and crossbreeding of the multitude.

Why is the multitude feared?

The multitude is the set of singularities: it must be dominated, transformed into a people. Ever since Plato and Aristotle, the people have always been perceived under the figure of unity. Yet certain philosophers, such as Machiavelli and Spinoza, sought to give a face to this multitude, to invent a politics of the multitude, to resolve the problems of common decision. It is a matter of urgent necessity that we reread Machiavelli and Spinoza!

You mention the problems of common decision. If a panel of ten people is asked to judge the quality of a text, for example, it is often, unfortunately, the most unadventurous opinion that wins out. In the end the decision is based not on the panel's shared enthusiasm, energy, and daring, but rather on the smallmindedness common to all its members. What is to be done?

Decision is the least of the problems we face, yet also the most complicated. Before reaching this stage it is necessary to understand the whole process of constituting the multitude, which is to say the construction of the commonality of a potential community.

One would have to devise a kind of sharing that retains the force of the singular.

This is in fact a fundamental question. Right now, for example, I am trying to figure out how to resolve the problem of war in this context. War poses in a paradigmatic way the question of what a real decision amounts to: the problem of war is decision. Now, in Empire, war no longer exists—war is finished. It may seem rather provocative to state the matter in these terms, but I sincerely think that the old form of war, nation-state against nation-state, war that inflicts death in order to defend borders, that sacrifices singularities in order to save a people—that this kind of war is over and done with. Clausewitz no longer applies. One must go back and reread Foucault's analysis of war, a quite stunning anticipation: it isn't a matter simply of overturning the Clausewitzian paradigm—it has to be turned inside out, like a glove. Empire is just this. The great problem today is to recharacterize war in an imperial context. How can war be waged today? Against whom does one make war today? And what is the difference between a world police operation—which is an administrative problem concerning management of the imperial space—and what the newspapers call "war"? This much is evident.

What exactly is evident?

The fact that we find ourselves in an Empire. But also the fact that, more and more, people are withdrawing from institutions—deserting them. They are turning their backs on power, they no longer want to be represented, they don't care. As Saint Augustine said, it is the City of Man that withdraws, not the City of God. The City of Man rejects adherence to power, to the norm, to the measure. There is, of course, a new nobility that has grown up around Empire; but all the rest, which is to say the great mass of people, the multitude that is free to move about anywhere in the world, that circulates in culture, that hybridizes itself—this mass is walking away. And so, one day or another, the multitude will indeed have to face up to the question of decision.

What, then, is the nature of the decision that needs to be taken in view of the enormous force of opposition it represents? How is this decision to be arrived at in view of the enormous tension it implies? What does it mean to reunite the multitude and invent other forms of life? The whole question of ontology is related to this. My dream is one day to have a chair of ontology!

We are now working on all these themes in the second volume of *Empire*. There will no doubt be discussions of power, new forms of organization, and a whole series of new categorizations. It will also be necessary to examine the different devices for reducing subjectivity, for dominating language and bodies. And there will be a major chapter on war—in other words, on what class warfare means, what war among nations means, how all these models are constituted, what type of war is typical of Empire today, and so on. There is also the question whether the forces of opposition can express themselves through war.

Does war necessarily imply hatred? Is there a decomposition of relations, as Spinoza would say?

Perhaps not. War is a great mechanism of decision—which may also be something dangerous. The problem is to determine whether war is a device for reducing the multitude to unity—nationalism, patriotism—or whether it may be something else, a decision of another type. I don't know.

But surely war implies the elimination of one of two protagonists, or else it will be necessary to conceive war in other terms—after the manner of Heraclitus, for example, as polemos.

No, it is not the Heraclitean *polemos*. We are seeking to understand the way in which war has been transformed into a device for imposing structure and order. The Heraclitean *polemos* is the upheaval of all forms; in Empire, by contrast, the capitalist system remains intact. Imperial war is not *polemos* because what animates it is a principle of order. Heidegger said something of this sort in connection with Heraclitus as well, but we know what inspired that interpretation. Heraclitus is not Parmenides in disguise. He is concerned at bottom with a kind of ontological war, whether it is physical, as with the atomists, or ethical, as with the Epicureans—in any case, it is a kind of struggle. In postmodern Empire, by contrast, war has been added to discipline and control as an instrument of government at the world level. Panic, fear, the feeling of insecurity—various forms of corrupted vitality—are among the elements developed by the bellicose function in Empire. We may also include television and the media in general: in this case, too, it is a question of elements that belong to a discourse that destroys moral consciousness and intellectual attention.

What, then, is the current form of war? It is a system for the production of order that operates through the destruction of society and of life. War is *arche*: at once the principle of movement and the principle of order—which is to say the contrary of what Heraclitus thought, and the opposite of what anyone caught up in war is apt to imagine. War is an overdetermination that strikes cultures with full force. But war is also a social phenomenon: a negative and destructive device, which leads to cultural and anthropological collapse, is imposed on the world of immaterial labor, on mobility and flexibility. Eugenics triumphs.

If one day *polemos* is reborn, it will have to pass through this terrible world; it will have to appear as a way of organizing revolt. Against eugenics, then, there is only *polemos*. But this must not be understood as synonymous with war—to the contrary, it is what constitutes the multitude.

F AS IN . . .

F as in Fascism.

There are some who say that fascism itself is also a form through
which the multitude can be organized. This seems to me incor-
rect: when the multitude becomes fascist, it has been led back to
the masses and to solitude. The multitude can become fascist
only when it has been emptied of its specificity, which is to say
of the fact that it is an ensemble of singularities, a multiplicity of
irreducible activities. Just like evil, fascism is always a negation of
power, a withdrawal from the common Being. The fascist
encourages hatred of the other, sanctifies violence as the remedy
for the vices of the world, obliterates differences, exalts the order
of a bygone world. Fascism—all fascism—reacts destructively
against the movement of life, against the joyous and multiple

manner in which it invents itself. Fascism is sad—it is the reign of coarseness and violence. Fascism is terrified, then, by the emergence of differences; scandalized by interbreeding, exasperated by alternatives to sexual pseudo-normality. Frustration, hypocrisy, and violence are at the root of all this, but there is something still more fundamental, more dominant: the fascist cult of identity, which forever renews itself.

But another phrase might be suggested for this letter—F as in Foucault-and-Deleuze—that implies exactly the opposite of what I have just said in connection with fascism. Because in Foucault, Deleuze, and a whole series of contemporary thinkers one encounters a discovery, deepening, and development of another heritage of modernity; a heritage that, instead of hiding difference behind identity and repetition, exalts it through the diversity of life. And even if the framework becomes more complicated, if we delude ourselves about the difficulty that a coexistence of differences sometimes involves, these differences are nonetheless subjected to the magic of time, with carries them away from any death wish. Foucault and Deleuze, each in his own way, reconstructed the free powers of invention in the twentieth century: they celebrated desire and identified as fascist all of the forces that stand in the way of desire and seek to block its emergence and expression.

G AS IN . . .

G as in Globalization.

In fact there are a number of themes beginning with G that come to mind: global (or antiglobal), Genoa, *guerre* [war]. We've already talked a bit about globalization and war. Let's pause for a moment to consider "antiglobal" and Genoa, since in any case they will lead us back again to globalization and war.

At Genoa there was an attempt once again to halt the cycle of struggles and the growth of the "*noglobal*" movement (as it is called in Italy). The police tried something both unusual and extreme: shooting a young man in cold blood. This was no longer a police action; it was war, or, more precisely, a low-intensity war combined with a high-intensity police action. Genoa—which I use as a shorthand for the defense of the Group of Eight

(G8) countries by the world's police forces—represented the highest point of institutional fascism: an implicit and organic fascism, consubstantial with the institutions being defended. All the usual reasons of state were advanced for this violence, including the most recent variant: "police science."

A new emerging cycle of struggles had to be blocked. Fortunately, the antiglobal protesters didn't fall for the trap that had been set for them. They responded instead by scattering first, and then later reforming in a procession. There were 200,000 of them; only one was murdered. Another 100,000 came the next day. What began as a demonstration against the eight major states became transformed into a demonstration against war—and this precisely at the moment when the G8 decided, in a sort of feverish anticipation of September 11, to add to the panoply of devices for controlling populations and movements, the formidable instrument of war. There was therefore an anticipation on both sides, by both the G8 and the antiglobal protesters. We found ourselves on the edge of war, and war did in fact come. Since then the state of war has been permanent: peace demonstrations are regarded as acts of treason, protests as acts of subversion—everything is potentially terrorism. Isn't this Genoa's message to us?

And another thing: with Genoa, the antiglobalization forces became truly globalized for the first time. The fate of a world destined by the G8 for war rested on the testimony of the *noglobal* protesters alone. These protesters thus became a multitude in every sense of the term and, for better or for worse, they were recognized as such: they became at once a subject of liberation and an object of repression.

One therefore cannot avoid the notion of war. It is necessary to emphasize once more the extent to which the Clausewitzian idea of war as the continuation of politics by other means has now been toppled, overturned, inverted. War has become the foundation of Empire. How, then, can we struggle against Empire? Everyone says "no" to war—but how can "war on war" be interpreted except as a duty inscribed at the core of liberation? The antiglobalization movement shows us the way out from the dilemma, the path of exodus: the encircling of power by the multitudes. It pits globalization against war, introducing and interposing itself between the belligerent parties. The antiglobalization movement is itself perfectly global. Will the multitude succeed in taking us beyond war?

H AS IN . . .

H as in Heidegger.

I remember when I first discovered Heidegger and began to read him. It was in the 1950s, when I was at university. One of my professors was an existentialist philosopher with links to Gabriel Marcel and French personalism. He knew the Germans very well, Jaspers, Heidegger, and the thinkers of the 1930s and 1940s in general—he called them "atheist existentialists." The faculty included scholastic philosophers who were interested in Heidegger as well. It was an exciting time, there was open and genuine discussion.

The Heideggerianism we knew was not pure by any means. It was part of a cultural milieu of Christian idealism preoccupied with suffering. All the authors usually associated with spiritualism, all the Russians, were present in this type of Western Christian thought—a curious Cold War amalgamation of writers, from Dostoevsky to Kafka, who appeared to have little connection with Christian spiritualism. In reality there was a great deal of theoretical confusion. And then there were the hard-line Catholics, Thomists who paid no attention to anyone else and who believed that the conception of Being in the great Greek classical tradition was fundamental, and that it had to be deepened. Here, too, there was a point of contact with Heidegger, though their conception of Being was nonetheless extremely different. For in Heidegger, of course, the linking together of causes does not lead to God, whereas in classical metaphysics, in the conception of Being upheld by the Scholastics, one always arrives at God. In both cases, then, there is a coherent system in which the Church—or, rather, the doctrine of the Church—is an instrument for maintaining order. In fact, this Being (whether or not one accepts the possibility of demonstrating it to be God) is essentially an ordered Being, with fixed characteristics. The infinite is not identified with an opening up. When one is operating with this conception of Being, Heideggerian thought winds up imposing itself in an almost natural manner. The only real novelty arises from all the linguistic aspects associated with the appropriation of the Romantic heritage, with anxiety and the concern for Being and so on.

Being as the guardian of Being—

Yes, all these elements actually belong to the moral aspect of this philosophical conception; but it is a morality and an ethic that have become, like all of Romanticism, the key to the interpretation of Being itself. In Heidegger's work of the 1920s and 1930s there is this fundamental intuition of Being in moral terms. And it is obvious that the conception of time, terrifying and obsolete, still remains marginal. The Heideggerian conception of time is a piece of folklore, a caricature.

Why terrifying and why a caricature?

Because there is this immobile, fixed Being—and time, which turns around it! And man's moral behavior, his position in this movement, is completely marginal. Man is caught up in time, but it is a time that is nothing, a continual revelation of being-nothingness. This being-nothingness is absolutely compact, destinal—it can't be escaped from.

Would you say that it is an antihumanism?

Yes. Above all, it is an extremely strong neutralization of desire, a marginalization and a neutralization: one is born of an act of destruction. This is an antihumanism and an antidesire—which is amusing, because this conception was already found among Catholics. In Pius XII, in the "Christian" fascists, there is an incredible resonance!

You know, there are some very strange circular (or perhaps spiral) patterns here: from Heidegger one goes back to phenomenology, from phenomenology to religiosity, from religiosity one comes back around to Heidegger, and so on. And even among the post-Heideggerians, among those who have sought to position themselves on the edge of Being through the Being/time/expression relation—I am thinking of Alain Badiou or Jean-Luc Nancy—here again I believe that one finds a very sharp turn toward mysticism.

This brings us to the late Heidegger and the poststructuralist posterity.

Heidegger wasn't the one who determined this posterity. But it is true that in structuralism there was a kind of turning back to Heideggerian thought: since structuralism lacked an ontological basis, it was natural to look for one there. I am thinking of the great philosophical enterprises represented by the work of Jacques Derrida and Giorgio Agamben; of all those who have sought to walk at the edge of Being, on its margins, finding a hint of ontological inspiration in these margins—the possibility of a return, a way back—whether it is a question of "differance" or of "naked life." These are quite different positions from a cultural point of view, of course, but I continue to sense in Derrida and Agamben the same tension and the same position in a direct line of descent from Heideggerian thought.

Ethical questioning in the work of these thinkers, as in that of Levinas, has become more and more mystical. It is a rather complicated discourse, one that goes back to the whole problem of choice and its consequences. One day it will have to be examined.

You seem to be utterly distrustful of this return—this sense we have today of being haunted, as it were, by ethics.

I am afraid that one constantly ends up transforming memories into memory. I am afraid of memory—for it is never something sharp or clear. Memory is always reconstructed: one always winds up being the prisoner of specters—or, worse, of ghosts.

In reality, we are ontologically reconstructed in relation to memory. By this I mean that what memory falsifies is restored to us in a physical and affective manner by our being. What is opposed to memory, then, is the irreducible and intimate dimension of the body. The body is never marginal, never a limit—and even if it were, it would present itself in any case as something that has experienced. It occurs to me to call this condition *eternity*—because it is not memory, but the body, that constructs being in a solid and irreducible manner.

But H also stands for Hybridization.

Yes—and it is this condition that makes hybridization possible. There are a thousand ways to hybridize Being, a multitude of ways to do it, because the atoms that make up the body are a multitude: when they combine with each other and with the multitudes of atoms that make up other bodies, a world is created. From this point of view the very principle of Being is one of hybridization. But there may be a still more obvious form of hybridization, when the spark of immanence is struck on the surface: white is crossed with black, and culture crossed with nature; biotechnologies hybridize cells, genuses, existences. I think that this world of hybridization, in disclosing what we are by showing us what we can be, by showing us our past in the light of our future, contains at once the reward and the risk of our ability to move about in the world. It is strange to note how many passionate debates and struggles take place today over this ontological and political hypothesis of hybridization. It isn't by chance that the becoming of Being must in one way or another be filtered through ethics: man's becoming is judged by man.

Nonetheless there are reactionary forces that reject hybridization altogether, no doubt because they consider Being as a *telos*—indeed all the fascisms of postmodernity cling to the idea of such a teleology. You will object that hybridization is a question of power, and that the majority of people who are wary of hybridization distrust it to the extent that hybridization is a form of manipulation or else is backed by a laboratory, a multi-national, or a lobby. I am perfectly aware of all this—I am just as concerned as they are by certain aspects of biotechnologies. It is clear that biopower has no intention of leaving hybridization in the hands of the multitude. But it is precisely for this reason that it falls to us to claim hybridization as a field on which to fight for freedom, and not as an extension of the subjugation, exploitation, and marketing of life. I say, then, that we fight on behalf of hybridization because we experience our own body as a hybrid—a little bit as the French may say, "We are all sons of immigrants." Even so, an enormous problem once again remains to be resolved: the confrontation between hybridization and democracy. Only absolute democracy is capable of permitting and explaining the multiplicity of singularities that proliferate in the commonality, and that are capable not only of organizing the multitude but also of laying claim to hybridization as a source of wealth.

I AS IN . . .

I as in I—the Self. Your thinking about memory leads us to the self, especially the unconscious self. Do you believe in the unconscious? What are these memories that you call "specters"? Does memory need to be exhumed, examined, put at a distance?

Above all it needs to be put aside! I don't know, I've never thought about the unconscious—though I have often said, by way of provocation, that I don't have one, which is perhaps true. In any case, if it exists it has to be discovered, and the problem is that when one discovers it, it's no longer there. This is a logical paradox. At bottom I believe that Lacanism is the only means by which the unconscious can be expressed.

The point is not to reify the unconscious, to describe it as an empty box that one peers into. Examining it depends on the technique of *Bildung*, of cultural, philosophical, and human construction in general. The unconscious is always formed by language, by the passions—why should one wish to make it reside somewhere? One can't point to it, one can't immobilize it, pin it down. It's always in movement, and so it can be defined only by acting and speaking—therefore it doesn't exist. Or else it exists everywhere. In any case I find no real reason to believe in its existence. I think a dismissal of the charges is in order, don't you?

I imagine you must sometimes have the impression of not coinciding with yourself, or that you experience Freudian slips or dreams that show your desire is not where you believe it to be.

But the fact of desiring something other than what one is capable of having is part of life!

No, that is another matter— there is no need of the unconscious for that. It's a question rather of an inner wound. Take the classic example of a person who has been abandoned in childhood and who finds himself abandoned over and over again in later life. He says: "The one thing I want is not to be abandoned and yet I always wind up being abandoned." And then he realizes, through analysis or by talking with a friend, that he brings it upon himself "unconsciously." This is to say, he does everything possible to cause the childhood experience to be repeated—though it is the opposite of what he desires.

I don't know what to say. The poor fellow! There are others who have been abandoned and who yet manage to pull through in life! What do you want me to tell you?

Surely you see that there is a discrepancy from time to time?

There is always a discrepancy. Life is such that we are constantly constructing and reconstructing what we know, through our relationship to others and the world. The problem of the unconscious is not to affirm *that* (which would almost be a banal truism in posthumanist experience); the problem is that if it exists, it needs to be substantialized—in every possible way: in an organic way, in a purely linguistic manner (taking into account its accumulation over time), even considering it as a pure void, in which case it must be situated, sacralized, blocked. At most, this unconscious is the very desire to live—which lands us back in banality.

Is there such a thing as a death wish?

I believe so.

This is the great Freudian premise—

The Freudian premise is a theological premise. There is an impulse to die that is opposed to the impulse of desire. The death wish is simply a limit, because Being does not manage to entirely express itself. Passion and desire seek to express themselves, but they run up against limits that, paradoxically, permit their construction—limits that must continually be exceeded. There is no impulse to go backward. It is always a process that pushes forward, even when one encounters limits. Evil does not exist, as Saint Augustine said once and for all. The ontological evil of Being does not exist.

Take the trial of Guy Georges, a serial killer—an almost perfect example of one, in fact.[13] How is this, this impulse to murder to be understood?

As an impulse to murder, not as a death wish. In prison I knew three or four true serial killers. The horrifying thing is that murder becomes the only way of surviving—or perhaps of living on after one's own death, I don't know.

I is also for Innocence: if one pushes your argument to its logical conclusion, one might suppose that there is only innocence. For if there is no ontological evil, where is sin to be found? It becomes difficult to conceive of responsibility.

Of course. The notion of responsibility needs to be understood as a responsibility of the spirit, the capacity that we have to live in common. My personal responsibility is a responsibility that I have in a process of community—what a horrible word: let's say instead a dimension where one is together; in Heideggerian terms, a *constructing-with*, a *constituting-with*. When one is in this process of community, one establishes forms of life and therefore, as a consequence, things that one can do and things that one cannot do. The sole criterion is the development of this

---

13. Guy Georges, suspected of having tortured, raped, and murdered seven women in the Bastille neighborhood of Paris between 1991 and 1997, was arrested in August 1998 after the largest manhunt in French criminal history. Georges was sentenced in April 2001 to life in prison, with no possibility of parole for twenty-two years.—Trans.

common, the liberty of being-together. There is no need to mythologize evil nor any need for a supra-human authority to guarantee the Good, whether a religion, an abstract ethics, or the state.

The Good alone does not suffice, alas, to guarantee itself.

But in the search for the Good there are instruments that we can construct. The problem is not to search for guarantees but to know how to construct. It isn't necessary to go look for guarantees outside of ourselves, outside of the possibility that men have of joining together to form the common.

But what instruments?

Rules of law, economic rules, rules of technology, rules of organization. In all the sentiments, in all the passions, there is a tension between the continuous invention of Being and the repetition of behaviors. At bottom it always comes down to the way in which one reasons, to what has been constructed by intelligence. We produce concepts, we produce names that are at once the result of a pooling of experience and a permanent integration of invention, of novelty. One sees this very clearly when one studies the development of children! If you look at how children learn, you see on the one hand that they are terribly conformist; but on the other that this conformism, which is at once practical and conceptual, is an open conformism. It continually integrates invention, discovery, production. And it is precisely in this way that the common must function.

I as in Invention.

Invention undoubtedly furnishes the most important way out from Heideggerian thought. For this death wish, which was a pure fantasy, was nonetheless expressed by the destruction of Europe, the end of the old Europe. I remain in agreement with historical materialism on this point. I think that the ideology of the dominant classes constructed its own coffin, not only in the case of Nazism, as is often said, but also through its exacerbation of nationalism, which spread this wish for death everywhere. I hope that we are finally going to find a way out from this whole period of our history, which was described by Thomas Mann among others; and from this whole literature through which we believe we have made ourselves when, in fact, we have destroyed ourselves! From this point of view, the most perspicacious observer was Stefan Zweig. His autobiography, *The World of Yesterday*, written during his last years of exile in Brazil, draws up a terrible indictment of all that. By itself it ought to be enough to prevent us from feeling any nostalgia for this time.

Why did it have such an impact? Was it a case of collective fascination?

I give the same explanation for it as the philosopher Lukács, which is to say the destruction of reason; or, more exactly, the destruction of reason by the bourgeoisie in the name of *their* reason. When reason began to be interpreted by other classes, the representatives of the bourgeoisie were so afraid that they sought to destroy reason in order to defend themselves. The working class, the intellectuals, the poor, the Jews, the persecuted had taken up the banner of the Enlightenment—this is what was unacceptable. The destruction of Europe was the destruction of the European ruling classes. All of postrevolutionary European liberalism, beginning with Louis-Philippe, brought about this destruction in order to prevent "the people" from taking possession of thought.

The paradox of this whole history is that since then production has become immaterial. This transition, from material to immaterial production, is essential: so long as production was material the bourgeoisie could maintain its power because it was easy to confiscate the instruments of production. But once production became immaterial—what we call the passage from Fordism to post-Fordism—two things changed radically: on the one hand, production penetrated all the way into the brains of workers, because in fact it is intelligence—imagination, the capacity for invention and creation—that is now being put to work; and, on the other, since the instrument is no longer the machine but the brain, confiscation by capital of the instruments of production therefore became impossible. One arrives, then, at this fantastic paradox: capital has won everything and, at the same time, lost everything. Today people have become the owners of the forms, the instruments, the tools with which they produce wealth. They no longer need to borrow their tools. For a long time wages were the payment one received for using the tools of others. Now it is the very concept of wages itself that needs to be reexamined.

A generation had been confiscated. The proletariat coped by transmitting an education to its children, but these values have disappeared as well.

The new hierarchical structure of life is founded on things that are not stable. In the constitution of Empire, a certain vertical mechanism for the attribution of values and the distribution of wealth has been established, but this process is not yet absolutely stabilized. This was rather clear in the crisis over the spy plane involving China and the United States two years ago. The Chinese won, because the United States ended up apologizing. War was not an alternative—in any case not *that* war—because the fact of the matter is that the Chinese can't be excluded from the integration mechanisms of the market. This was a horrible thing for the Americans to have to admit, horrible for all the bosses of the world—but blackmail is now no longer possible. It is absolutely necessary that the Chinese elites be integrated in the process of globalization, in the world game of control: they can't be avoided. It is therefore no longer the Americans against the Chinese, but the world capitalist elites against no one and everyone at the same time.

The creation of a new hierarchical order is under way, and for the moment nothing is stable. What we are witnessing is the establishment of a new law. To be sure, the world elite decides, but it never considers itself responsible at the ethical level. If anti-AIDS medicines are expensive in Africa and deprive an incalculable number of people of the possibility of surviving by slowing the effects of the disease, the world elite limits itself to saying that this is an economic consequence, an effect of hierarchy, without anyone ever feeling a sense of responsibility. Everything has become blurred. How then are we to struggle? The apparent disappearance of the adversary is the great problem today, as much for those in power as for all those who wish to try to resist them. Nonetheless there is always the possibility of withdrawing. Of choosing "exile," or, more exactly, an exodus that is not necessarily spatial—leaving for somewhere else is not always possible; in that case a logic of eluding power is the only practical and effective form of resistance. What is unfortunate is that while we can probably afford the luxury of such resistance, Africans may not be able to—

Able to leave Africa?

No, to leave everything. Since we can, the logic of escape still remains for the moment a privilege.

There is a moment when choice is no longer possible—this is perhaps the ultimate form of subjection. It is also a question of survival. Have you ever experienced this in a particularly intense way?

There is, of course, the experience of survival in the strict sense: that is to say, surviving with the memories of what one has already known and lost, where one experiences this survival as something empty and useless. But there are also moments when one feels oneself to be a "strong" survivor, a *résistant*, and in this case there is a very considerable positive element that comes into play. One may survive and resist at the same time, which was my experience.

During my first years of exile in France I initially had the impression that everything was finished—I was a sad survivor. It was a time where I was faced with naked life—I was completely abandoned, I no longer knew where I was. Yet at some point I rediscovered the possibility of true resistance—a bit remote, but possible just the same: as Galileo said, the world turns! *Eppur si muove*—it moves. Resistance exists. Once one has realized this from a purely private point of view, one manages sometimes to discover ontological levels of resistance. One manages to grasp the existence of a gamut of possibilities beyond oneself, renewals of life, desires that change and that depend on one another, on survival and on collective resistance. There are, for example, different levels of consciousness—indeed of life, of desire—that are intertwined with one another. In the case of strict survival, one is reduced to certain elementary necessities of life, although in survival through resistance there is an additional dimension that is first and foremost the expression of a positive and common desire, a desire to construct together.

If one thinks, for example, of the relations we have with lovers, or of the bonds that we maintain with our children, it is rather clear: in simple survival, one is at the lowest level, in a sort of static state preserving what already exists, where the need is to preserve everything one has, not to lose anything—because any loss would threaten the little that one has left. In the case of resistance, on the other hand, life increases, intensifies. One might even say the same thing about sexuality. In simple survival, one lets oneself go—one is at the limit of deprivation and one seeks simply to preserve oneself. In the relations of resistance, by contrast, new forms of life are produced and invented.

J AS IN . . .

J as in Jamais plus—*Never again. When you think of the phrase "never again," what is the first thing that comes to mind?*

Never again war! I was two years old when my father died in 1936. He was an active member of the Communist party. The Fascists made him drink castor oil, which is a little like drinking dirty motor oil. It causes considerable damage, blood poisoning and so on—it literally empties you out. That was how he died. The family was unalterably opposed to fascism. And then my brother died as well—he was seventeen, I was ten. Padua was bombed a dozen times before we decided to flee. Afterward we took refuge in the countryside, but there was bombing there as well. There was a bridge nearby that the Allies pounded every night and that the Germans always rebuilt the next day.

Being antifascist and having a brother called up to serve the
Fascists must have made it all the more terrible.

You can't imagine the madness and pain of this period. My
brother died on the front in 1943. He had enlisted, God knows
why—he was an adolescent when he signed up; he wasn't even of
age. My aversion to the idea of the nation probably stems from
this experience. At home we were antifascist, but just the same it
was necessary to defend Italy: what did one more contradiction
matter? And so the other thing to which I'd like to say "never
again" is the nation, patriotism—all these snares and delusions.

   The next year, in 1944, the man who was to marry my sister
came into our lives. He was a Communist partisan from the
mountains, an Italo-German born in Trento. He's the one who
raised me, a sort of very young surrogate father. His family lived
in the Dolomites, which is where the first partisan brigades were
formed after September 8, 1943, when the Italian army was dissolved following the surrender to the Allies and the king's flight
to the south. Mussolini's regime had collapsed in July. By early
September, Italy was under invasion by the Germans, but the
Allies had begun to land in Sicily. All the antifascists regrouped in
the mountains to fight the Germans, who occupied the north of
the peninsula. My brother-in-law's brother was an air force officer—he was a fascist, and the partisans were ready to punish him.
So my brother-in-law, who was a young medical student at the
time, went up into the mountains to plead for his life. The partisans said to him, "If you want your brother to stay alive, you'll
have to stay with us." They took him hostage because they needed
doctors and he knew something about medicine. This is how he

became a Communist! Up there in the mountains, among the partisans, he met wonderful people, whom I later came to know myself. It was an experience that marked him for life.

And his brother?

His brother was a foolish young man who wanted nothing more than to be in the air force: the image of the "pilot hero" had a certain mythical appeal at the time. His plane had been shot down in Libya and he was given a medal. My brother-in-law finally sought refuge with us since his brigade had been wiped out in the mountains. He stayed the whole winter of 1944–45. Then he left because as a partisan he was a wanted man. He had to go into hiding again. My brother-in-law—I was twelve, he was twenty-four—was one of the two people who initiated me into Communism. The other was my paternal grandfather, a wonderful character who meant a great deal to me as well. My grandfather was a worker who sought to escape the poverty of the countryside in the late 1890s by moving to the city, to Bologna, where he worked on the old horse-drawn tramways. He joined the local socialist organization and became an important member of the union cooperative. Still today I have the right to live in one of the apartments of this cooperative—it's a hereditary right so long as you continue to pay the union dues. This was one of the first cooperatives for workers in the building trade. My grandfather then became a night watchman in a bank in Bologna. Summers I often went to see him. He passed the time telling me stories of the struggles. I was brought up with those memories, yet I don't think I ever once experienced a moment of elation; nor did I ever feel conditioned by this family history, either negatively or positively. It was simply part of my life.

But even so, being brought up with these memories must have left its mark.

For my grandfather, education meant transmitting the history of the struggle against all traditions—because for us tradition meant the tradition of slavery, of forced labor, of poverty. One can't imagine what it was like to get up every morning at five o'clock and carry a hundred pounds on one's shoulders the whole day. My grandfather hated this work because he had first-hand experience of the physical and moral alienation it entailed. This is a far cry from alienation in Sartre's sense! I think that the whole family was marked by this idea, even if we chose different paths. My brother-in-law, the ex-partisan, became a radiologist, but he lives only for the mountains—this is his way of remaining faithful to what he was. He's an honest person. My sister is a neuropsychologist who studies the localization of functions in the brain. She's an excellent biologist, a respected academic. They are both very dear people who have supported me enormously. They've never ceased to be Communists—nor have they ever forgiven the party for sending me to prison. They have shown much love to my children and taken care of them while I was behind bars. They have withstood every test.

But isn't memory necessarily on the side of tradition?

Who controls memory? Faced with the weight of memory, one

must be unreasonable! Reason amounts to eternal Cartesianism. As against Descartes, one ought to choose Galileo instead: the most beautiful thing is to think "against," to think "new." Often memory prevents revolt, rejection, invention.

And so your grandfather transmitted to you a heritage and a memory against tradition.

There is no reason I should tell you that, but I'm revealing myself completely!

I observe that children raised without any experience of the transmission of an oral and collective memory, which is to say a memory rooted in the body, incarnated—like the one your grandfather transmitted to you through his accounts of struggles—produce among other things a lamentably conformist American-style bourgeoisie. What spurred you to revolt? Was it perhaps not these very tales your grandfather told you, which are not only a memory but which also transmit what you call the "common"?

Perhaps. But I've also seen people filled with the memory of struggles who were great fools. In the 1960s and 1970s, for example, the Marxist-Leninists were lamentably rigid—to say nothing of the Trotskyites, though they were perhaps a bit more likeable. For the most part they were fed by the same memory, but that didn't make them any more intelligent or open! This continuity of memory, this habit of thinking in traditional ways, quickly becomes dogmatic and persists. In philosophy, and in practice as well, it is difficult to free oneself from it.

Descartes managed to.

Yes, but philosophers use instruments that are extremely sophisticated. When these same instruments are put into everybody's hands the results may be unsatisfactory. It's obvious that nothing is more widely shared than common sense, but the effects of a philosophical critique of tradition are not immediate! What is needed is a political critique of tradition. Oppression is founded upon tradition, the Church is founded upon tradition. This is what people have to think about, what they have to react to.

Wasn't your grandfather fascinated by Russian communism?

He had grown up with the myth of Russian communism. My father was one of the founders of the Communist party in Italy, but old Enea, my grandfather, never joined. I believe he always voted for the party, but he never became a member. My grandmother was a seamstress and made shirts by hand. She was very cautious when it came to politics. Her main concern was raising a family. She made a crème caramel the like of which I've never tasted since. To be honest, I've never been particularly fond of sweets—I prefer salty to sweet—and I don't care much for Proustian reminiscences. But in the case of my grandmother's crème caramel, it's the sugar and the involuntary memory both—I wish I could be clearer, but this is what it was. Her crème caramel never left me any choice: my memory of it is above all one of pleasure! Isn't that what Proust was saying? Negri the Proustian! That's rather funny, really—but there you are.

elation; nor did I ever feel conditioned by this family history, either negatively or positively. It was simply part of my life.

But even so, being brought up with these memories must have left its mark.

For my grandfather, education meant transmitting the history of the struggle against all traditions—because for us tradition meant the tradition of slavery, of forced labor, of poverty. One can't imagine what it was like to get up every morning at five o'clock and carry a hundred pounds on one's shoulders the whole day. My grandfather hated this work because he had first-hand experience of the physical and moral alienation it entailed. This is a far cry from alienation in Sartre's sense! I think that the whole family was marked by this idea, even if we chose different paths. My brother-in-law, the ex-partisan, became a radiologist, but he lives only for the mountains—this is his way of remaining faithful to what he was. He's an honest person. My sister is a neuropsychologist who studies the localization of functions in the brain. She's an excellent biologist, a respected academic. They are both very dear people who have supported me enormously. They've never ceased to be Communists—nor have they ever forgiven the party for sending me to prison. They have shown much love to my children and taken care of them while I was behind bars. They have withstood every test.

But isn't memory necessarily on the side of tradition?

Who controls memory? Faced with the weight of memory, one

must be unreasonable! Reason
As against Descartes, one oug
most beautiful thing is to thin
memory prevents revolt, reject

*And so your grandfather transm
ory against tradition.*

There is no reason I should tell
completely!

*I observe that children raised w
mission of an oral and collectiv
ory rooted in the body, incarnat
transmitted to you through h
among other things a lamentabl
geoisie. What spurred you to re
tales your grandfather told you,
which also transmit what you c*

Perhaps. But I've also seen pe
struggles who were great fools.
ple, the Marxist-Leninists were
of the Trotskyites, though they
For the most part they were fe
didn't make them any more in
of memory, this habit of thin
becomes dogmatic and persists.
well, it is difficult to free onesel

Descart

Yes, but
ticated.
hands t
ing is m
a philos
needed
upon tr
what pe

Wasn't

He had
father v
but old
voted f
mother
cautiou
a famil
tasted
sweets-
Proust
crème
both—
crème
above
Negri
are.

So joy, for you, is also a crème caramel?

Yes—you have no idea what it was like. In our home it wasn't called a crème caramel; we knew it as *fior di latte*. It wasn't until I had a crème caramel at a restaurant when I was older that I realized my grandmother's wasn't the only one.

J as in Joy . . .

Joy is an expression that finds a response, an act that is added to another, that connects. Even when it comes to joy one can never be mystical. For me mysticism is the worst thing there is, because there is a negative foundation that one thinks one is escaping, only to fall back into it. In mysticism, joy is the disappearance of suffering. Now joy can, of course, be understood as the opposite of suffering; but for me it can't simply be defined as a lack of something, because joy is also something full, something positive. Joy is the power to create—overabundance, excess. In fact, it is the only definition of God that I am prepared to admit: overabundance, excess, and joy are the only forms through which God can be defined.

Therefore we are able to participate in it from time to time?

The problem is not the participation but the construction. One participates to the extent that one constructs something in common. Joy is directly related to the perception of this "common"—to its power. At the same time there is nothing transcendent in any of this.

You don't conceive of joy as something that exists all by itself.

No, I can't. I don't think anything exists "all by itself"—not even language, not even the minimal linguistic awareness that allows us to say that we exist. The fact of existing, as an act of recognizing one's own existence, is a matter of recognizing one's own speech and implies a linguistic community. The linguistic community is extremely strong, indeed perhaps one of the strongest communities of all. A Spinozist analysis of the linguistic community is needed. For Spinoza, language is bound up with the passions. I think of the great literary and philosophical tradition that produced this idea, from Rabelais to all the current poststructuralist linguists, who are finally beginning once again to speak of the language of the body. And it isn't by chance that one of the themes that recurs in this philosophical tradition is laughter. Laughter is the intermediary form between language and the expression of passion. It tends toward joy, obviously. Think of the laughter of the child. It would be interesting to know to what extent a child's laughter is already speech.

There is a whole group of poststructuralist thinkers who hold that structuralism missed speech as body, notably in connection with the question of rhythm, rhythm as median. Rhythm, laughter—there are a number of Russians who are working on this theme at the moment. It's an idea that I've been toying with for a while as well. I may end up doing something on it.

K AS IN . . .

*K as in Kant. When I suggested this you said, "Oh no, I hate Kant!"
Is this true?*

No. In fact I've studied him a great deal. The part of Kant I like
the most is the least Kantian: *The Critique of Judgment,* which is
to say aesthetics, the active transcendental functions. This is an
admirable work. It marks a critical moment, introducing what
Kant called the transcendental schema of the imagination. The
notion that the imagination has a duration—that the constructive imagination falls within time—is absolutely modern. And
even if Hume had grasped it before him, Kant remains important because he isolated the transcendental function, which the
idealists later made a shambles of. The third *Critique* is really the

joining together of the thought of the Enlightenment and the heritage of a certain English philosophy.

What seems to you creative in this definition of the imagination?

The fact that the forms that one projects upon reality to understand and organize it also have the capacity to construct something new. This leads us back once again to language and its creative capacity; to the moment of ontological community—or the ontological "common" that is revealed by language. From this perspective, what I call *kairos* is an exemplary temporal point, because Being is an opening up in time; and at each instant that it opens up it must be invented—it must invent itself. *Kairos* is just this: the moment when the arrow of Being is shot, the moment of opening, the invention of Being on the edge of time. We live at each instant on this margin of Being that is endlessly being constructed.

But this isn't the margin that Heidegger speaks of—a margin of Being, the margin of the instant where it happens, or rather the margin of the impulse?

The instant that creates is the instant where Being creates, but it can be blocked by our inability to accept this opening. What I am trying to describe through the idea of *kairos* is not Bergson's *élan vital*: positing a temporal continuum doesn't suffice to describe the process of the creation of Being.

In other words: if one stops, it stops.

Yes, if one doesn't keep pace with time, it stops. Time is something that one interprets, that one folds—something through which one is carried. But it is not a blind power.

It exists, nonetheless, outside of us.

Yes, in the sense that belonging to *kairos* is never solipsistic. Many others are part of it as well. If you think about it, our whole corporeality works in this way. Only death can destroy this relation between the body and *kairos*. It may become necessary one day to repeal death. This isn't a new idea, by the way—it was first proposed by Descartes.

And why not? It's not unthinkable a priori. *Just so,* kairos *is both the after—what comes next—and language.*

Kairos is the way in which one sees the world, a point of view—one that is also a view of the past. The past is reconstructed on the basis of *kairos*, but it is not the past that constructs *kairos*. And to the extent that it is *kairos* that reconstructs the past, no access to a pure past can be had.

One must nonetheless be careful, because when one says there is no pure past there is a risk of falling into a sort of total historical relativism. In reality, however, once a thing has been said, I cannot undo it: it has been said; and once a thing has been done, I cannot undo it: it has been done. *Kairos* confirms that to us, puts it in circulation. Hospitality is not only a matter of opening one's arms and saying, "Come." It is also taking the other's arm and saying, "Let's walk together." It is this circulation, this sharing, that is terrific, wonderful. The classic, Spinozist idea of friendship involves constructing ever more complex and stronger levels of Being through the encounter with different *kairos*. Every time an encounter takes place there is a construction of Being. In the Judeo-Christian conception, a restoration of Being is the most that one can hope for. One must therefore take part in this hope—

But isn't this the same as constructing?

Construction and *kairos* walk together. In *kairos* there is the idea of living labor. Living labor is what constitutes the reality of the world: it is a bodily *kairos* that generates a physical and mental energy. *Kairos* is productive. Indeed, it is a production that fills the whole of life—a bioproduction, a biolabor. It is the opposite of dead labor, which is negativity itself: what *is not*. It may seem a bit paradoxical to battle against something that doesn't exist, but it is the only possibility of overcoming that we have.

L AS IN . . .

L as in Lombard. What is the "Lombard spirit"?

Lombardy is a region in the north of Italy located between Piedmont and the Veneto. I say "Lombard" in the same way I might say "Venetian." I am speaking of the spirit of the plain of the Po. It was there that my mother and her family were born. These were people who had a religion of the land—small farmers, neither poor nor rich, who worked enormously hard in order to be able to eat white bread. Their olive oil bread is unforgettable. Being Lombard means having a sense of the land, but also many other things that these quiet and free people invented. The Lombards invented money. They conceived the idea of commerce very early, by the end of the Middle Ages—and the end of the Middle Ages, in Italy, was two centuries ahead of the rest of Europe. The exchange of merchandise meant organizing commerce throughout Europe, along the sea and the rivers: from Italy to Provence via the Rhone, and from Provence to Spain and Catalonia; along the Rhine as far as Holland; and along the Danube. These three rivers were the main thoroughfares of expansion for the Lombards. From this point of view I have a deep sense of being Lombard—a sense of mobility that doesn't exclude an attachment to the land, because these merchants always came back to their native region. They brought Italian artists along with them on their travels. And when they found men of unusual talent among the foreigners they met, they brought them back to Italy. There was this great exchange, then, which was at once commercial and cultural. The land along the Po is completely flat; it is black, and so rich that it yields two or three harvests a year. It isn't even known when the first irrigation systems were devised. They are probably mentioned in Virgil.

Yet there was a time when it was a very poor region.

Yes, but in the central part of the plain, as far as the foothills of the Alps—from Ferrara to Modena, and from Reggio Emilia to Parma—the poverty was not so severe because the land was fertile. People came through after harvest time and gathered up what was left: this was enough to eat for six months. There is a whole art of living in Lombardy. This is one of the best places for eating in all of Europe. They invented tagliatelli, tortellini, parmesan, Parma ham. They're incredibly hedonistic. And the family is no more than a very formal structure—perhaps you've seen Bertolucci's *1900*! A great many human passions are found there, a very beautiful, sweeping language, a spirit of community that reflects the Po itself—an uncontrollable river along which people have always worked together in order to prevent or otherwise avoid floods. The spirit of community is therefore very strong, with all the defects that this inevitably brings: people are born together, they eat a lot, drink a lot, make love a lot. There are veritable tribes among them—it's a very beautiful thing. It is this capacity to work together and to invent relations that produced commerce. Not modern commerce, but rather a form of exchange where one asked others what they needed and worked from there. Wealth was created and administered. Women ruled in the home. They dominated family life and even had a certain degree of sexual freedom. Crimes of passion were very rare. Today all that seems to have profoundly changed. The last decades of the twentieth century have destroyed the generosity of people and replaced it with hypocrisy and egoism. This strange transformation can't be explained by the rejection of a sudden modernity that caused the "local" dimension to disappear and that bureaucratized administration. There was a federalist—perhaps even separatist—revolt, movements against immigrants that were sometimes overtly racist. I have tried to understand the reasons for these protests, both in Lombardy and in the Veneto. It is obvious that there are many things the people of these regions do not like: they pay higher taxes than other Italians, for example, although the level of services and so forth that they receive is very low. But there was a sort of leap into the void, a deterioration in their civic behavior, with the result that their revolt, understandable at the beginning, took an extreme and brutally violent turn.

You find them changed?

Yes, because of liberalism, because of the Right. For a hundred years, from the birth of the Italian Socialist Party, Milan never had a mayor who was not a man of the Left. Under fascism, Milan and Bologna were always governed by the Socialists—"fascist Socialists," but men of the Left just the same. Municipal administration never changed in the major cities of the north. They were run by Socialists, then by Communists, then by Socialist-Communists; but since 1970 there has been a great change of direction because all these parties eliminated the only possible way for the Left to be truly on the Left, which is to say by integrating new movements into the struggle. They refused to take into account the new social and political situation. Instead they turned in upon themselves, rallying around an inflexible ruling class that was incapable of thinking. It's no accident that Milan, and a little bit later Bologna, ended up going over to the Right. Bologna had been known for years as "the Red"—you can imagine what a shock that was! And why I have fond memories of the gentleness of Lombard life and the communal spirit the people of the Po once had!

M AS IN . . .

M as in Multitude. This is a word you often use.

Yes, I have already used it a number of times in the course of this abecedary, particularly in relating the idea of Empire to that of multitude. But in discussing the concept of multitude itself, one must keep in mind that it has three distinct senses. The first is philosophical and positive: the multitude is defined as a multiplicity of subjects. Here what is being challenged is the reduction to unity, which is to say the permanent temptation that has poisoned thought since classical metaphysics. The multitude is, by contrast, an irreducible multiplicity, an infinite quantity of points, a differentiated—an absolutely differentiated—whole. Do you really think an entire population of citizens can be reduced to unity? That is absurd. The multitude of singularities cannot be reduced to the idea of a people. During the modern period "the people" represented a hypostatic reduction of the multitude: sovereignty claimed to have its basis in the people and transferred its image to them. The deceptions of political representation were woven with the concepts of sovereignty and people. But where, then, has the sovereign people gone? It is lost in the mists of Empire, voided by the corruption of representation. Only the multitude is left.

In the second place, the multitude is a concept of class: the class of productive singularities, the class of operators of immaterial labor. This class is not itself a class—it is rather the creative strength of labor as a whole. Multitude is the name of an economic reality, still subject to the vagaries of a power that would like to ignore the transformation of the labor force; business managers frankly say that only war makes it possible to guarantee and assure a productive future. But if this labor force is no longer a class, it is nonetheless an extremely strong productive force. The struggle of the working class no longer exists, but the multitude proposes itself as the subject of class struggle: to become this subject, it must be the most productive class ever invented.

Third aspect: the multitude is an ontological power. This means that the multitude embodies a mechanism that seeks to represent desire and to transform the world—more accurately: it wishes to recreate the world in its image and likeness, which is to say to make a broad horizon of subjectivities that freely express themselves and that constitute a community of free men.

M as in Matter . . .

Let me reply by posing an impudent question: what does matter think of me? Thought is too often opposed to matter, just as thought is opposed to life. But thought is not something different from the rest of life, nor from matter.

Is there a "matter" of thought?

Yes—matter's the matter.

What is matter? No one knows what it is. What is Being? That seems to me mysterious.

Idealists and all those who believe in God have a very clear idea of what matter is: it is the opposite principle to that of God; the opposite of the truth, of what is beautiful and good. Matter, in Plotinus, is nothingness. The universe thus becomes something quite bizarre, because idea must always be mixed with matter in order to exist—Being must be mixed with nothingness. If we deny the consistency of matter, and the fact that it is what is, we fall into one of the most sophisticated forms of philosophical stupidity. The only real mystery arises when Being is defined as something different than matter, as irreducible to the set of determinate connotations that form matter. Matter is free: atoms rain down on the universe and in this way constitute it. Only a *clinamen* can intervene here, which is to say the freedom that is inherent in matter and that makes it hybrid. In addition to the truth of ancient materialism, we have the philosophical power of Spinozist materialism, according to which matter is conceived as a body, and the body as a power that raises the plane of immanence to a height at which it can declare itself divine. All teleologies fail because they ignore matter; and because matter is the depth of the affirmation of man's freedom of man. As a consequence, linear or dialectical teleologies that prefigure the models and measures of the future disappear. Materialism is the affirmation of life, without either theoretical mystification or political authority. Materialism is always revolutionary, because matter is revolutionary as well.

M as in Monster . . .

The monster breaks with theology. Montaigne said that God has no interest in the monster. Even Montaigne, who was nonetheless a great innovator in relation to classical theology, was afraid of what the idea of the monster implied. Which was what? That the metaphysical and ontological mechanism is not based on measures and prototypes but, by contrast, on freedom, on *kairos*, on the body and its capacity for invention and self-invention. Thus world is made, and made for this reason: it is the cause of itself. It is power.

This frightens us, because it gives free rein to every sort of fantasy.

Of course—above all, at the moment, to fantasies associated with biological engineering, even if the problem isn't actually new. It was raised earlier by nuclear engineering. Here one touches upon one of the great questions of existence: hasn't man always dreamed of being God since he was free to think? It is amusing to note that, from a philosophical point of view, this temptation was felt even by reactionary thinkers such as Plato, Aquinas, and Hegel. One finds it everywhere because it is the source of man's very desire to think. Today we've actually reached the point of playing God. We have finally attained an incredible power that used to belong to the domain of literary anthropology and that is now ours: metamorphosis. Matter, and the monster, can be mastered through *kairos*. Matter can be recognized as *kairos*, and the monster can be recognized as the possibility of metamorphosis. Once again, as with every open possibility, one finds oneself faced with a terrible ambiguity: who will rule on this matter?

Machiavelli said: "An assembly of those who know."

Machiavelli said many things. In particular, he said that the only possibility of constructing and interpreting the common is to experience it as a democracy. Machiavelli understood democracy as the capacity to express oneself without passing through unity: that is, as an expressive phenomenon. I am more convinced than ever of the fact that metamorphosis is a radically positive phenomenon, so long as one treats it as a democratic decision about the common. One can't have groups of experts that evaluate and decide the metamorphic development of man: only the multitude can decide at the moment of metamorphosis itself. Bodies can decide only once they have accepted the operation of metamorphosis, but they must accept it in common: they must decide it in deciding reasonably what mankind wishes to become.

Who will decide that the metamorphosis of humanity is good, that it creates new figures of life— or that, by contrast, it only furthers the cause of eugenics?

Under present circumstances, which is to say global capitalism and the shortage of democracy that we see around us today, it is far from clear how experimentation on life could produce anything but a generalized formatting, a "race of slaves"—

Human beings who would serve, for example, as a reserve supply of organs?

Alas, we didn't have to wait for cloning to discover that certain people are considered to be nothing more than spare parts. But yes, this is more or less the idea. The thought of manipulating the genome is frightening. We are at a point where one might suppose that the history of humanity is over. Man must reassume responsibility for all this. It used to be said that revolution was necessary: this is an old and completely stupid slogan, but today revolution has once more become fundamental. It remains to decide who is capable of bringing it about. It is up to us to decide.

But who is to decide? And on what grounds? How could a decision be made without reproducing a hierarchy? You suggest that one of the objective criteria would be a certain maturity of judgment. Once again we find ourselves faced with the prospect of a council of Platonic sages.

No—the people who participate today in this process are people like you and me, and our children.

But look at the scientists and their ethics committees. Scientists are consumed by a passion for knowing, and so they pursue their research at all costs— the appropriation of the living world by science seems quite irreversible.

Ethics committees are interesting, but of limited effectiveness. Things would need to be worked out in such a way that decisions are taken in a collective and practical way. This is said to be the crux of democracy—but the problem is that the term "democracy" has been emptied of all its meaning. Democracy is said to be identified with "the people"—but what is the people? It is said that one must go back to the model of the classical *polis*—but that has nothing to do with the modern conception of democracy. This is really a quite unbearable situation. Such confusion cannot be allowed to go on. The real questions must be posed. We are now living in an age where the problems of life, of power and of politics have become central and indissociable. It is from this fact that we must start over once more.

Is this why you think that the monster is a new figure?

Yes, because we must decide which monster we want. The monster is the *angelus novus*. But in Benjamin this angel was looking backward—the Communist revolution, looking back over a landscape of destruction and terrible struggles. The *angelus novus* was this new tragic figure, the symbol of those who wished to continue the revolution even though they knew it was impossible. Today the *angelus novus* has become the politics of the monster, the desire for the monster—which is to say the hope of being able finally to reappropriate life for oneself in all its power, in all its creativity. The multitude must democratically decide the future of man.

N AS IN . . .

N as in Naming. Why is the act of naming so important?

Naming is at once the Bible and what makes epistemology possible. How does one go about naming things? Naming consists in putting together common elements, things; but it quickly becomes clear that this amounts to no more than naming parts. When one limits oneself to naming parts one becomes lost in an infinite process and in reality names nothing. One decides nothing.

The alternative is to proceed by intuition: naming what one finds, what one identifies. But it is difficult to believe that everyone names in the same way. One finds oneself faced, then, with the problem of knowledge and the transmission of ideas.

Naming must therefore be a collective and common process. You mentioned the problem of decision—naming is perhaps the only process through which a form of decision can be imagined. It involves two elements: the first is that everyone agrees; the second that this agreement leads to a decision. The formal condition for this process, in other words, is that everything be common and that in this commonality there be a moment when a decision is actually taken. This implies another formal condition, then, having to do with the time it takes to reach this moment. The problem is how these two formal conditions can be embodied by a multitude that has become common.

N as in Negri. Sometimes your name must have functioned as a common noun?

I have sometimes tried to distinguish between Toni Negri—object, common noun—and Antonio Negri—philosophical author. But it is a complete illusion. From the beginning of the 1960s until my arrest in 1979 I clung to this distinction. The "professional," philosophical books were written by Antonio Negri; the rest, the political books, came out under the name of Toni Negri. In 1979, with the arrest of Toni Negri, this became a difficult distinction to sustain. Every evening the eight o'clock television news led with a picture of me—big nose, bushy hair: the horrible visage of the "wanted" criminal, the *cattivo maestro*, the wicked teacher. And that went on for months and months. On television and in the papers there was always some excuse for running a photo of me. In 1997, when I came back, I had no end of trouble trying to get them to stop using this horrible picture.

That must be oppressive.

One gets used to it. One absorbs the blows, like a boxer. The hardest thing was enduring their accusations: imagine being accused, as I was, of having killed seventeen people, business-men, journalists, policemen—even a magistrate who was a very dear friend, and who came to my house for dinner a few days before he was assassinated. It was claimed that I killed all of them in cold blood. In the case of Aldo Moro I was said to have been recognized by witnesses. My voice was formally identified as that of the person who called the Moro family on the tele-phone to negotiate. Eminent linguists confirmed that it was in fact me—one of them recently became Minister of Education. It was dreadful.

How did you respond? Did you disprove the accusations?

The decisive testimony, as it turned out, was given by a "peni-tent." He'd gotten half of the Red Brigades arrested, and he finally explained to the judges that I was an enemy of the Red Brigades—that they had condemned me to death. It's difficult to admit, but this man saved me.

I didn't realize you'd been specifically accused by name. I thought that you'd been accused of inciting people to murder but that the allegation was not made against you directly.

No, to the contrary, it was absolutely direct: I was accused of being the military and ideological head of the Red Brigades: the mastermind—the one they called *il grande vecchio*, the power behind the scenes.

Did they really have a mastermind?

No, only in their imagination. But the obsession still resurfaces from time to time. Recently they said that it was an orchestra conductor no one has ever heard of who lives in Tuscany. The problem is that they needed to believe in a mastermind, a leader. They couldn't imagine that the *brigatisti*, who for the most part were very young, had managed to do what they did by themselves. For the authorities, it was absolutely obvious that they had been either commanded or infiltrated, and that therefore someone had done their thinking for them.

The accusatory mind is always paranoid.

It is paranoid because it is effective. There is a need to demonstrate the impossibility of doing possible things. The power of institutions is based on habit and the absence of resistance. It is therefore necessary to show that spontaneous resistance is impossible. Television, detective films, a whole certain literature shows a force of the state at work that doesn't exist. The only thing on which the state rests is the lack of resistance, passivity.

That makes me think of Subcomandante Marcos in Chiapas and the blindness of intellectuals, in Mexico and elsewhere, who thought that he was not important because he defended only Indian culture. But what is interesting about Marcos is precisely that he represents spontaneous, collective, yet nonetheless organized forms of forces of resistance. And that is what bothers them so much—that they can't point to a leader, an ideology, an oppression!

Nor was there a true leader in Italy; and in any case, Toni Negri had nothing to with the Red Brigades. To come back to the question of names: when I think of myself, I think of Toni. At university I was Antonio—yet everyone called me Toni. It's as if I didn't have the courage to call myself Toni all the time. I don't know why. Perhaps because at bottom I thought that there were different levels of writing, and that the distinction between Toni and Antonio allowed me to acknowledge this. By 1979 this kind of subtlety no longer had any justification. In everyday life, in any case, everyone calls me Toni. Only certain Mafiosi from the south called me Antonio, in prison. I think that for them it was a sign of courtesy and respect.

Does this distinction between levels of writing still hold today?

I don't care. They can call me what they like. There was a moment when Toni Negri and I parted ways. I would read his name in the newspapers and not realize that they were speaking of me, there were so many horrible things this man did. It may be that Antonio is the name that is closest to me, a sort of false name. I don't know.

Perhaps there is no such thing as a true name?

Perhaps one has to look for it, construct it. Perhaps the two names are signs of something else. But all that is a game that after a while becomes tiresome. In life one is often someone different.

One is a multitude?

The multitude is an infinity of singularities. It is because I am not in myself a multitude that I aspire to construct it with others. Or else it is the opposite: it is because I am a multitude within myself that I wish to find the common of the multitude outside myself.

N as in Neutral. . . . What place do you assign to the idea of "neutralization"?

Neutralization is always negative. If one considers the world as the stage on which history plays itself out, and history as something that is always organized by forces and energies, then if one wishes to destroy that stage it becomes clear that in fact this is impossible. At most one can try to neutralize the relations of forces, to make them cancel each other out. This is what we are now seeing in a period of profound change: an attempt to neutralize new energies, new forms of life. This is a profound innovation on the part of power, a truly bold strategy: systemic neutralizations by which a force is opposed to its symmetrical and inverse counterpart in order to reduce it to zero; enveloping neutralizations that strike at the heart of certain phenomena in order to paralyze them. In reality the process of neutralization operates by moving itself between a systemic economy, which is to say the idea of a system of forces, and an antagonist economy, which is to say a specific finality of eliminations. In theory it is a problem of teleology and measure. It is necessary in any case to realize that the forces today that lead to innovation, to thematic change, have become very powerful. Neutralization is therefore obliged to make itself odious, because to be effective it always needs a surplus of violence, an overdetermination of terror. This is why at the present moment war comes to complete the sequence of discipline (of individuals) and control (of populations), and goes beyond the modern definition of power.

Even if neutralization is disguised, it is always violence.

Yes, this is a real problem. When one realizes that the biopolitical world is dominated by the multitude, the thematic of neutralization becomes more important than that of sovereignty, if only because it is more effective. That means that the legal instruments involved in the juridicalization of life become essential, particularly in their procedural form. To say that juridicalization has replaced sovereignty amounts to affirming that procedure has become more important than norms. In reality, the objective can no longer be the elimination of the adversary but, at most, its neutralization. What is at issue is the fundamental passage from discipline to control: this is exactly how Deleuze read Foucault's analysis of power. It is no longer a question of discipline but of supervision.

But now we're talking about something else. Power as a process of crushing resistance is the form assumed by neutralization today.

No, not crushing—at least not always. There is an infinity of possible forms of indirect, invisible neutralization. The conflictual, antagonistic relation is no longer straightforward but complex, perhaps because it has now become difficult to identify which subjects confront each other: there is no longer such a thing as Power with a capital P—only powers, or, more precisely, relations of power. There is no longer a single subject of resistance, but a multitude of subjectivities—which brings us back to the difficulty of naming: I continue to refer to the "new proletariat" because I still do not have an adequate name for the new subjects of the multitude.

This is why naming is a revolutionary act.

The opposite may also be true. The new subject is a "monster"— a hybrid, invented creature. The absence of a name is inconvenient, but it also has a certain usefulness: normally, to name means to identify; and identification is the first step in the neutralization of this force of collective and nameless invention that is the multitude.

The new form of opposition, I believe, is invention/neutralization. It will be necessary to try to find a way to name the new thing without neutralizing it. Once again one comes back to the problem of *kairos.*

O AS IN . . .

O as in Oppression.

One no longer knows where to look for oppression. In a standardized society such as ours, perhaps it has been too much talked about—one has seen oppression everywhere and one now finds oneself suffering from a kind of mental block regarding its definition. It's obvious that there are new forms of oppression: new forms of immaterial oppression, for example, that act upon workers in the new technologies and the service sectors, or that derive from the flexibility and ferocious mobility of the labor market. The big difficulty is that it is no longer possible to identify a specific form of oppression capable of provoking an equally specific form of resistance. Perhaps the term *oppression* should be replaced by *exclusion*, or perhaps by *destitution, suffering,* or *poverty.*

It is difficult to struggle against an invisible enemy.

It is precisely this that one must learn to do: to struggle against an invisible enemy, against a non-identifiable oppressor. If one is faced with invasion by a foreign army—

Yes, that's easy—

No, it's not easy! It's now become extremely complicated. The same army drops bombs, propaganda, packages of medicine and supplies: liberation or oppression? The army grants itself the right to interfere: liberation or oppression? The army alternately makes use of non-governmental organizations (NGOs) and rejects their assistance: liberation or oppression?

Armies today are reduced to a police function. This is a remarkable perversion. Global policing operations are even acclaimed by international popular opinion. Conflict between sovereign states is now a thing of the past. The NGOs that struggle against oppression are so certain of the values they uphold that one begins to wonder. Some NGOs make me think of the mendicant orders of the late Middle Ages. I have great personal sympathy for the Dominicans, for example, who truly tried to help people, the poor, the suffering. The fact remains, however, that they were absolutely convinced that they possessed the truth, which means that they, too, were perfectly capable of waging holy wars—crusades. One can't say that the Franciscans and the Dominicans were bad sorts: they chose poverty and endured it fully, admirably. And yet here again it is a question of affirming a certain truth. In the same way, the behavior of NGOs that believe they are liberating people sometimes has terribly perverse effects. I think we must find a way to see the irony in peaceful armies, primordial rights, interference and non-interference: not for the pleasure of demythologizing NGOs in an abstract way, but because everything has become incredibly complex. I am neither a skeptic nor a historicist—I simply think it is necessary to redefine oppression. On the other hand, oppression is also the daily bread of millions of persons—it's what prevents living, breathing. The small oppressions of everyday life—

Do you struggle against them in your own life?

I'm asthmatic—the difficulties of breathing are very familiar to me! Laughing is the best form of resistance!

In any case the majority of human beings live constantly under some kind of pressure, whether material, mental, or physical. And perhaps it is this set of pressures that materializes us individually. Each of us can be defined by the set of pressures to which he is subject and against which he reacts. The great problem is to free oneself from all these things—to escape from the "generic anonymity" of oppression, to give it a face.

Generic in what sense?

Oppression is so nebulous that it can't be named, so diffuse and so gray that responding to it is hard. We must find a way to dispell the fog of oppression, to invent new alternatives.

P AS IN . . .

P as in Panic. Panic has to do with oppression. Perhaps panic is the extreme state of an event that causes it to erupt.

Panic seeks escape from the multitude, and disaggregates it, with two possible and equally catastrophic results: absolute individualism and mass phenomena. It is necessary to understand this panic—which is everywhere today, particularly in the financial world—and to combat it.

Is it a new, latent form of panic—

It comes from a feeling of insecurity, from an abandonment of the god Pan, the fear of seeing all the values in which one has believed, the values on which one has constructed one's whole life, suddenly collapse—the fear of the void, the fear of innovation. One might say that panic is the total absence of *kairos*: one finds oneself on the edge of the void without being able to throw positive bridges across it, against it. It is the vertigo of the opening, the terror of creation that confuses the absolute void with the possibility of novelty. Perhaps panic substitutes today for the fear that Hobbes described as giving rise to the contract of association that provides the foundation for the modern state. In *Empire* we tried to bring out these aspects. In the fear of man against man there is still, at bottom, a certain longing for peace. For Hobbes, the contract represents political peace. In panic, by contrast, there is no longer even a longing for peace but simply the desire for a certain kind of normality, even if for this reason there must be war. Panic is linked in particular today to new forms of financial organization. It no longer affects only the rich but also the middle class and, increasingly, the working class, which is similarly inclined to gamble the money it has saved for retirement in the stock market. In the United States, for example, the majority of the money invested in mutual funds comes from retirement plans. Financial panic therefore becomes something that is directly related to people's lives. In the modern period this fear was at the root of the contract with the state. But in the new postmodern and imperial situation in which we find ourselves today, panic is the basis of the demand for imperial authority: everyone wants things to stay the same. And because panic arouses a clear desire to neutralize all sources of conflict, peace itself becomes passive, inactive, submitted to. Perhaps in panic there is even a certain demand for oppression. After all, oppression is rather practical—so long as circumstances are bearable there is no need to take decisions.

In addition to financial panic there is also social panic, which is to say the feeling of insecurity. Insecurity is quite obviously an element of financial panic, but it is necessary to go beyond this and take into account especially the social panic of the poor, the destitute, which includes the fear of not being able to pay the rent, not having enough money to get to the end of the month; the terror of overdrawing one's bank account, of having the electricity and the telephone cut off, of not being able to afford a cup of coffee. In the last decade these threats of insecurity have become the fundamental weapon in the blackmail practiced by the Right, and sometimes even in the discourse of the Left. In this way the fear of insecurity gives way to fear of immigration, and then to stupid and dangerous protest votes. But the problem is actually much greater than this, because it isn't limited to the electoral terrain: we are currently witnessing a castration of the species to the extent that violence has been introduced into biopolitics, that the world of desire has been crushed. The feeling of insecurity and its political causes, as they are manipulated today by capitalist elites, therefore represent not only a political weapon but a kind of hybridization in reverse: a tendency toward ever greater misery, toward the destruction of desire, toward the erosion of life. Margaret Thatcher was the heroine of a base and terrible moment in the history of ontological destruction.

P as in Prayer. Haven't you ever found refuge in prayer?

The unconscious has unquestionably played a certain role—an altogether stupid one—in my life: when I am afraid, I sometimes

think of my mother or of the Virgin Mary. This is a bit of superstition, something that I've done since I was little. Prayer and
superstition are very closely related. In Italy people are very
superstitious: they are forever identifying good or bad omens
and trying to maneuver between them. My children are even
more superstitious than I am. My older daughter made a very
fine short film a few years ago that won a prize at the Locarno
Festival. It tells the story of a girl on a big bed, in the middle of
the sea, who awaits her lover. He is swimming toward her from
very far away. The wait seems endless. In the meantime a succes-
sion of bad omens besiege the floating bed: black cats, three
nuns, and so on. The girl prays, wails, implores. Then, in the
midst of so many symbols of misfortune, a great storm comes
over her and her raft. In the end the exhausted lover arrives after
all. It is a dreamlike, hilarious film, but very poetic as well. It is a
film about fear.

*For you, then, prayer is associated with extreme situations—some-
thing you resort to in the face of anxiety.*

Yes, it is effective when one awakens during the night. When I
was in prison, waiting for them to grant my petition for parole,
I was afraid it would be rejected. During the day I managed to
control my anxiety quite well—I told myself that everything
would turn out well in the end; but during the night, at three or
four o'clock, I would wake up in a state of torment. Then I
would think of my mother.

And what did your mother say?

Oh, she didn't say anything in particular! She calmed me down.

So she was a true mother!

Yes, from that point of view she was marvelous. She was already old when I went to prison. We wrote long letters to each other in which she told me everything. She died in 1982. Between 1979 and 1982 she wrote me every week—we never stopped talking. My mother was an extraordinary woman. She understood the importance of freedom. She let me go abroad all alone, hitch-hiking, when I was fifteen, at the end of the 1940s. I went to England with very little money when I was still in high school. It was enough that I said I wanted to learn English. She let me leave on the condition that I would write. We didn't have a telephone. In any case I didn't have enough money to telephone.

And your trip to England went well?

Yes, I worked and traveled, hitchhiking around. Afterward I hitchhiked often. I traveled everywhere this way until I got married: throughout Northern Europe, a part of central Europe, North Africa, the Middle East. . . .

And so leaving is associated in your mind with the idea of liberty, of discovery.

Yes. It's strange, my desire to travel has waned a bit. When I was young I was fascinated by civilizations, by archaeology; a bit less by nature, although I was very sensitive to landscapes. I have trouble understanding people who shut themselves away in vacation clubs in the Maldives. I've become a little lazier. There are still parts of the world that I don't know, or that have undergone such upheavals that I no longer know them: the former Soviet Union, China, Latin America.

Latin America, for example, is a genuine civilization.

Yes, unquestionably. Yesterday the rector of the University of Bogotá was here, and I asked him many questions. He told me that in the Andes everything needs to be built or rebuilt. It's a huge undertaking—the complexity is frightening.

In reality, we must begin to understand that on the flat surface that has been marked off by Empire there is no longer any chance of connecting political thinking with evolutionary theory and the theory of states. Now the danger of this was already clear from historical experience: one had only to look at the way in which colonialism and imperialism made use of this connection. Marx himself thought that the history of mankind had been preceded by that of the apes, and that it was necessary as a consequence to bring them up to the level of men. Unfortunately, the rupture represented by evolutionary theory and the leveling of the conditions of human life manifested themselves in the worst possible form: the neoliberal managment of global capital. But in a world in which merchandise and information enjoy absolute freedom of circulation, the singularity of common—communal, cooperative—experiences emerges on an egalitarian plane that knows principles neither of hierarchy or of evolution and that seeks global expansion. It is not by

accident that Chiapas has entered our world—which is to say
our reality as well as our imagination, our communication, and
our language—as an essential element. We ought therefore
always consider ourselves as interlocutors with each other. It's a
bit like the nature of prayer, which we recognize also in political
anthropology: in both cases, the appeal occurs on a plane of
immanence, on a surface rich in singularities—precisely the one
on which we find ourselves today. It is there that we would like
to recognize peace.

But what is peace understood to mean today?

It seems to me that peace is always related in a certain way to
war. But in an imperial world such as ours, without any possible
"outside," the question may have no answer. Peace and war in
effect have exchanged roles: war has become a force for order,
while peace seems to be one of disorder. In this world without an
outside, war and peace can no longer be outside one another. It
is this hybridization of war and peace that needs to be analyzed.

Inquiring into the origins of the modern state, at a moment
when the paradigms of sovereignty and the nation-state were
being formed, Hobbes described history as the continuous
attempt of humanity to find a way out from the state of war. At
the same time he saw sovereignty as the guarantee of peace.
What one used to understand by "peace" was therefore clear: the
possibility of surviving, which was paid for dearly since it meant
being alienated from liberty. War was the negative condition of
peace—a form of blackmail forcing the choice of alienation. The
modern state was thus born in going beyond war through war:

the Thirty Years' War represented the birth certificate of modern sovereignty, which is to say peace. But what kind of peace could be hoped for after so much pain? Traversing a landscape of massacres on the cart of Mother Courage, who could have imagined that peace would ever come? How could one of the thousands of Simplicissimi[14] born during this war have conceived of such a thing? Peace became an ideal preceded by so many misfortunes that no one any longer really knew where to look for it. Between 1618 and 1648 Germany lost half of its population. When peace was achieved in the modern state, it had already become a utopia. This, then, is the first paradox that we have to confront.

Has war in the postmodern era become a force for order?

Yes. Whereas in the modern era peace was an ideal to be attained (or, more exactly, a regulative idea), today the idea of peace resides within the idea of war. War is the maintenance of peace—the voyeurism and the police force of peace. Here, then, is a second paradox. The relationship between war and peace that obtained at the beginning of the modern era has been reversed: peace is no longer the solution to war, not even an ideal or a utopia; it is now a simple procedural condition that is internal to war. One therefore is faced with an absolutely unprecedented original situation, which no longer even corresponds to

---

14. The reference is to Hans Jakob Christoph von Grimmelshausen's novel *Der abenteuerliche Simplicissimus Teutsch* (1668), which tells of the life and misfortunes of the peasant Simplicius Simplicissimus during the Thirty Years' War.— Trans.

the maxim *si vis pacem, para bellum*—"if you wish for peace, prepare for war." Today one finds peace only in war. But what kind of peace are we talking about? What order is left to this word *peace* now that it has been emptied by war? In postmodernity, sovereignty no longer offers itself as an instrument for extracting peace from war. Instead it is the capacity to mix war and peace indiscriminately.

All modern literature, when it speaks of war, depicts a moment when man finds himself alone on the battlefield. What one finds—in Grimmelshausen as in Tolstoy, in Stendhal as in Céline, in Remarque as in Hemingway—is a man who is either wounded or who has miraculously survived, but who in any case is stupefied by what has happened, and still more so by the fact that the moon and the sun are still able to shine. The return to peace is a sort of natural restoration, a restoration of life. But how are we in our turn, in postmodernity, to imagine peace? Can we shield it from the monstrosity of war? Or is peace itself altogether as monstrous as war? Where, then, is peace still to be found? The desire for peace no longer seems to have any natural basis. This is because peace has itself also become monstrous. Under these circumstances we await something unforeseen—a new monster perhaps—that can free us from the ordinary wretchedness of peace and war, which are now mixed together in the new imperial order. None of us is able any longer either to imagine or to describe a battlefield after a massacre, or capable of being surprised at still being alive amid the conjuration of death.

"They make a desert and call it peace"—thus Tacitus. But this view had been expressed earlier by Thucydides. Historians are more realistic than poets. They feel no hesitation in considering brute force as a lever of political order. Machiavelli starkly recounts fierce plans of war devised in order to obtain peace. Peace, he tells us, is always imposed. Peace is a value that only war makes possible, merging realism and cynicism in an absolute way. But is the claim that war can create order still valid today, or is it now necessary to suppose that it too has become, in its turn, a simple illusion? The answer is not rhetorical, because it insists on the reality of this illusion. In the world today, war, peace, and barbarism are mixed together and feed off of one and the same history. The great pacifisms—whether Christian or communist—contemplate a sacrifice for the purpose of constructing peace, and therefore are linked to the modern idea that peace and war are successive and/or separate moments. But today it is precisely for this reason that they are no longer able to embody an effective project of peace. There is no longer any place for pacifism. The only resistance to war possible today is "war on war."

We are no longer even capable of desiring peace. But what does it mean to speak of "war on war"?

In this situation, in this new hybridization of war and peace, this world without an "outside," one can only attempt exodus—an exodus that leads nowhere. By "exodus" I mean constituent power: exodus and "war on war" don't signify the same thing. It isn't enough to withdraw from the world market; the market itself has to fall apart. This is exactly what the implosion of imperial institutions currently taking place shows us, namely, that it is not by accident that Empire is always a synonym for corruption, which is to say the contrary of generation. Before being destroyed by terrorists, the Twin Towers were weakened by this indistinctness between peace and war. The terrorist attack was horrifying, but it only aped the methods of imperial sovereignty. The kamikazes of September 11 existed in this type of sovereignty. What difference is there, then, between all these terrible rituals of war that ceaselessly answer each other in an endless symmetry? Perhaps the image of the Renaissance hero, who knew both how to fight and how to legislate, to produce art and to define a new world, may help us to lift our flag out of the mud—the flag of peace, which is to say the emblem of a pacified reality. Perhaps it will permit us to dominate illusion, allow us once again to traverse the wastelands and swamps of Empire. Can such a thing be imagined? Or is the chaos too great? From now on peace is no longer a condition of life: it can only be reinvented. It belongs to the exodus from the world that the City of Man attempts to construct.

P as in Passion—human passions, political passions. Is passion the place of maximum intensity at a given time?

Yes, that's true. But passion is not only the maximum intensity: it is perhaps also a cold continuity, extremely intense, but—

What do you mean by "cold continuity"?

When I think, for example, of the amount of energy we needed to slowly construct, over decades, a low-level organization in the factories, this was a cold passion. It required time and self-discipline, a controlled excitement, a certain patient wisdom.

But then this is no longer passion at all, if it is controlled—there is no longer the passivity associated with the etymology of the word "passion."

Passion is also a form of life. There are two fundamental elements in the definition that I give of passion. There is tension toward the object, the desire that this object—an ideal, utopian object—be present in life. Often I use the phrase "self-deconstructing utopia" (*désutopie*) rather than "utopia" precisely in order to cool down this tension, to render it more conscious. But passion also signifies, ontologically, to construct: passion constructs Being. When one experiences passion, one constructs scenes, horizons, structures, desires, and joys, both for oneself and for others. Passion leads always to the common: this is why terms such as "betrayal" and "wound," which signify the dissolution of the common, are ontologically so charged.

In the case of amorous passion, one has the impression of being outside the world.

No, that is something else—what you psychoanalysts call *folie à deux*. True passion is a common construction, at once within the couple and outside it. It is this openness that is moving in true passion: a feeling of power, a desire to create—that operates through procreation as well, through children—which is to say also a desire for community, sharing, cooperation. I have never believed that the public must be sacrificed to the private, or vice versa, because I have never believed that these are opposite terms. When you meet someone who understands that, it becomes a fine love story, a story full of life, full of desire. For me, the return to Italy also coincided with the renewed desire for a love of this kind.

There is a certain romantic ideal of the couple, a partnership that is closed in upon itself and that endures even if all other forms are tending toward expansiveness.

I have never accepted that. All the great loves that I have experienced proved the opposite. When I married for the first time I was twenty-seven years old. Our personal project was also a political project, a true declaration of both private and public morality against the hypocrisy of the stereotypes about the family and the couple. It wasn't a question of anything goes. We had a different project: we were struggling not only against social oppression but also against the forms of oppression conveyed by traditional notions of the family. Nor was it enough simply to wish for freedom. The problem was to make this freedom productive. The traditional couple is never anything other than a repetition of the social order. Each time that I've lived with a woman we have succeeded in inventing a new project. This is what passion is: something that opens up, that anticipates *kairos*. Perhaps here again it is a question of the role of decision—a theme that is so noticeably missing in my work, yet upon which everything in it converges. In this case decision amounts to a short-circuiting of passion, to a sort of instantaneous time—a sudden opening of time onto the void and a passing from thought to action.

Q AS IN . . .

Q as in Questioning. Is the problem of decision ultimately one of questioning the world?

It's obvious that we have the duty to think, to question, but there is a danger of giving into a certain temptation to prophecy—of believing that one has all the answers. An Epicurean or a Stoic ethics is worth more than all the prophetic moralities together. I completely disagree with provisional moralities of the Cartesian sort, because a provisional morality can exist only in a theological world in which truth is something other than what we do; and because beneath a provisional morality always lies an absolute morality.

What would an ideal morality be?

According to Descartes, we would be able to know this only once we have attained a position of certainty. So long as we do not reach certainty we do not arrive at a point of decision—we must restrict ourselves to a provisional morality. But I disagree. It is true that when one arrives at small moments of decision, at small *kairoi*, at small joys—all this is singularly important. It is perhaps true that the love of God is more important than the love between two persons. But the love of two persons for each other is an extraordinary thing—a singularity, an awareness of existence, a construction of being where before there was nothing. From this moment on, love exists: something has happened. How do you expect a provisional morality to take that into account?

Is it the act that makes it happen?

Yes, it is the act. The act achieves its effect through passion, through community: it comes from a kind of metaphysical cooperation, from a mutual impulse, a genuine opening up. Every moment that one is alive one creates. Each moment is a creation—except for moments that one cannot really experience, where one is so neutralized that life becomes a parody of itself.

"Love of God"—does that have any meaning for you?

To say that one is in God is, at bottom, very Spinozist. One is in the substance of God. But the noblest thing is that each day one creates God: everything one does is a creation of God. To create new Being is to create something that, unlike us, will never die. Everything that we do enters into eternity. The beauty of Spinoza's thought consists in just this: the divine is not outside us. Power in Spinoza is not the same as in Bergson. For Bergson, power exists outside of us; for Spinoza, it is not the force of a physical process, it is the whole difference between modern and ancient materialism—between Spinozist materialism and Democritean or Epicurean materialism. If you consider another great figure, Lucretius, you find yet another notion. Lucretius conceives the moment when Being is created as something that happens in the universe. To be a Spinozist, by contrast, means to believe that it is given to us to experience this moment of innovation and to accede directly to eternity. We are the *clinamen*, the particular angle at which atoms fall in the universe. We are the ones who determine all this. I am convinced that it is not philosophy that teaches us this materialism of freedom, but instead social struggles, the great movements—the practice of life.

R AS IN . . .

R as in Resisting.

The resistance of the multitude to all attempts to format life consists above all, I believe, in experiencing the pleasure of singularity. Arriving at this conception was very difficult for me. I had read Spinoza. But it wasn't until I began to read Deleuze, and then to discuss his work with him and to reflect upon it more deeply, that I understood the intensity of this concept of singularity. It involves much more than the singularity associated with the movement of Being because the infinite is experienced entirely in each singularity; that is, the act of life is totally internalized. This is not the same thing as vitalism, since forces are no longer admitted. It much more closely resembles musical notes, which, although they are completely singular, are capable of creating life, of combining with each other to produce harmony. When I say harmony I do not mean a measure—because one can always change this measure—but each particular moment of life. I don't know whether Deleuze actually worked through this idea to the end or whether I only wish that he had. In its innermost depths Deleuze's philosophy is very much in the French tradition. I fought a lot with his students and friends, because they laid enormous emphasis on all the Bergsonian figures one finds in his thought. To my way of thinking it was necessary to insist instead on the constitutive power of singularities, their power to constitute the common. For the singularity always points toward the common: the common is its product; and singularities arise from the proliferation of the common. I believe that resistance consists in just this process. There is absolutely nothing organic about the common and its resistance: as Deleuze reminds us, the singularity always stammers. But this stammering creates a common world. The singularity doesn't deny the stammering—it enriches and articulates it. Resistance is the meaning that the common offers to singularities.

R as in Return. Was your return to Italy secretly an act of resistance?

When I went back to prison in July 1997, to the Carcere di Rebibbia in Rome, I did not exactly go back to Italy. And even when I was allowed to work outside during the day, beginning in September 1998, this wasn't really a return. Italy, and Rome in particular, seemed to me difficult to understand. My return amounted to exchanging one place of exile for another. I was still awaiting the moment of my return. Arriving in Rome by plane after fourteen years of exile in Paris wasn't enough: something quite different is required if one is truly to speak of going back. At the present moment, four or five years later, I can just barely begin to describe it. Return ought to be a sort of reconstruction—not a re-seeing, a re-living, or a re-remembering, but a construction of something new, a new foundation of life. Somewhere earlier in the course of our conversation I said that the absence of memory seems to me ethically preferable to the stubborn search for a past and for one's roots in it. Coming back, setting foot on ground I thought was familiar, I didn't have to try to recall this old idea of the absence of memory: it imposed itself upon me with considerable force, because I didn't recognize what I found there. Everything had changed, everything had become uglier—and the change had caused passion and hope to disappear. Only my public image had stayed the same, like a millstone around my neck: I was still the *cattivo maestro*, the wicked teacher of the 1970s, thirty years after the proletarian assault upon the state. I realized then that this image was fixed for life—as if my entire existence was doomed to remain forever petrified in the past. And if that was the case with my enemies, it was also to a certain extent what I experienced with my old friends, whose uneasiness sometimes gave way to unbounded loyalty, sometimes to suspicion. Often the same people loved and hated me both. From this point of view, my return had perverse consequences.

In order to break the spell I had to search for the reason of return not in the past but in the future—to come back in order to construct. And this turned out to be the direction events actually took. Two events brought Italy back to me, but paradoxically neither of the two took place in Italy. The first was Seattle, the second the worldwide success of the book that I had finished in Paris with Michael Hardt before coming back to Italy. These two events catapulted me out of the past and restored me to a position on the front lines. I can assure you it was a powerful experience—a little like Baron Münchhausen, who lifted himself out of the gutter by his bootstraps. I had to come back in order to be there, to act. It is only when friends begin to smile at you again, and enemies fear you again, that you regain your place in political and social life. Return is therefore not only a coming back but also the effort and joy of being back: of being there rather than somewhere else. It is the joy of rediscovering not community and roots, but linguistic innovation and the freedom of the passions. Even remembrance and memory can be recovered when you are once again immersed in ontology, in being that is at once the past and present of life, in the determination of being-there. When the Genoa events took place, this wonderful (and successful) uprising of the multitudes against the "Great of the Earth"—then and only then did my return truly have the taste of reality.

I believe that return is always something personal, which varies according to the person and the circumstances; but there is a sort of transcendental form of return, which must find a suitable matter in order to be able to affirm itself as real return. For many of those who came out of the concentration camps, for example, the true return was probably the construction of Israel. For Italian exiles under fascism, it meant constructing a republic and engaging in social struggles on behalf of communism. For the rest of us who made 1968, coming back meant constructing something the possibility of which we had glimpsed in the 1970s, and which Genoa confirmed for us last year: the new forms assumed by political subjects and of the communist process. Return is the term that succeeds in mediating resistance and the future—more precisely, that projects resistance into the future through a dislocation of time and space. Return, for me, was like moving a knight on a chessboard.

S AS IN . . .

S as in Sensuality. Does one think with one's senses?

I believe one does, yes. The senses are fundamental. I have never
worked on the senses as such. I am not convinced that the classic inductive doctrine of materialism, of radical empiricism, is
the only satisfactory one. There is a profound interactivity
between reason and the senses. From this point of view I am a
Kantian, not in the analytic sense but so far as the transcendental schematism is concerned and the possibility of constructing
"bridges" between the senses and reason, between the world and
the imagination. I don't believe that the senses by themselves
furnish a basis for knowledge, or for the faculty of judging and
acting. Vulgar materialism, which enjoyed a considerable vogue
in the guise of Soviet dialectical materialism, seems to me now

at last to be finished. Appallingly foolish things were written in its name in the last half of the twentieth century. The great heroes of Soviet materialism were d'Holbach and La Mettrie—they hardly deserved the honor! When I was young, twenty-five years old, I worked on the German materialist psychologist Fechner and on the tradition that linked him to Gehlen, but I had to abandon these studies—there wasn't time for everything. These authors nonetheless left their mark on me.

What interests me is living experience, and I came to it through the philosophy of Spinoza. All Spinozism is a philosophy of the senses, since it is a philosophy of the body. It is the senses that open us to the common. But to speak of the senses is also to speak of my experience of prison, of a life deprived of sensuality—not only of erotic sensuality, but of the use of the senses generally. In prison one loses the sense of depth perception, since one's line of sight is always cut off by a wall. One forgets what it's like to walk on the ground, because for years one walks on cement. When I got out of prison the first time I went directly to the home of Claudia Cardinale, a very dear friend who lived in a very beautiful villa outside Rome where I was finally able to walk on grass, after four and a half years of concrete. I had the impression I was walking on rubber. I'd forgotten that when you walk on the ground you are not walking *on* a surface—you are walking *in* the surface.

Then there is the sky, the only depth that exists when one is in jail: it is an immense pleasure to see something fly across the sky—a bird, an airplane—and the traces it leaves behind. One can survive being locked away in prison only if one has great passions; if one preserves the ability to create a powerful imagination on the basis of this empty *kairos*. For me this powerful and new imagination had to be reconquered from within the very heart of defeat. It's for this reason that I read a great deal of Leopardi and wound up devoting a book to him; also the story of Job, whom I want to write about as well.

Why Job?

Because the story of Job is marvelous! Job is really the theory of the vision of the inside of desire—a desire that contains its object: my God, I have seen you, therefore I possess you. It is this access to God, this suffering that is so terrible that paradoxically it makes it possible to possess the object of one's desire under incredible pressure, and with incredible passion. There is a moment when Job says: "Until now you have done with me as you have wished, you have ruined me, I no longer have anything, and everyone asks me if I still believe in you. Well, yes, I do still believe in you, because I want you, because I want to see you." It is an act of tremendous pride, an exemplary fable! Job is the opposite of the defeated and exhausted figure that the Church sometimes offers us: he is able to bear the pain of his suffering and his downfall because he has this tremendous ethical—and, above all, theoretical—capacity to construct the object of his desire. Even for an atheist morality the story of Job offers a way of making sense of the history of Judaism and Christianity. Spinoza said the same thing in the *Tractatus Theologico-Politicus*, where he described the religion of the Jews as the construction of a desire, the invention of forms of community. The human invention Spinoza describes could be constructed in all religions. If there is any interest in studying religions it can only be to understand how an object of desire can be constructed and generalized. We ended *Empire* with a reference to Saint Francis of Assisi, because he seemed to us to symbolize the new militancy of our times. And everyone said that all these references to religion were rather "New Age"—

Religion isn't "New Age"!

I've never had anything against religion—I'm simply against transcendence. I absolutely reject all forms of transcendence. But certain aspects of religion, and above all certain religious experiences, truly have the capacity to construct, not only in a mystic way but also in an ascetic way. Asceticism has always fascinated me: it is an internalized construction of the object; whereas mysticism, by contrast, is a distancing from the object— a negative theology, a theory of the margins. Asceticism is a constituent state, a transformation of the senses and the imagination, of the body and reason. In order to live well and to construct the common, asceticism is always necessary.

Christ-like incarnation is a kind of ascetic guidance, or rather a path toward the virtuous life—as Spinoza recommended. It is probably in secular asceticism that singularities and sensuality are most effectively intertwined in order to construct the world to come.

T AS IN . . .

T as in Temptation.

A marvelous phrase occurs to me. Michael Hardt and I were discussing the definition of the concept of multitude, and Michael cited a passage in the Gospels on the temptations posed by the devil. The devil appears, saying that his name is "legion": "We are a legion of devils." This story is fascinating, because what is expressed, bizarrely, is the possibility of multitude. That's not a bad introduction to temptation—a legion of devils! Above all, it is a way of affirming one's desire to possess all possible wealth, all possible virtues and powers. In the theory of angels, whether they are fallen or not, everything proceeds by legions: cherubim, seraphim, and dominations, the highest order of angels.

This summer I was going to reread Dante's *Divine Comedy* with a friend who is a philosopher and a professor of Italian literature. He has entirely reconstructed Dante's philosophy and revealed, in particular, the influence of Duns Scotus upon it. Dante knew of Duns Scotus and his doctrine of *haecceitas*, or thisness. From this point of view Dante is a Deleuzian philosopher, because the divine world is one of singularity: the spectacle of a multitude of singularities. The concept of singularity as it is worked out in Deleuze is essential for understanding the passage to the postmodern; and the most incredible thing is that it is already present in Dante. To come back to temptation, it must be recognized that it is quite agreeable to swim in a sea of temptations. Perhaps temptations are nothing other than the modes of this substance—the desire to do everything, to love everything, to know no limits. I speak of "modes" in the manner of Spinoza when he says that modes are like the waves of the sea. Temptation is a call from the world: one must know how to hear it and how to accept it. The problem is that there is always a price to be paid: in the case of temptation by the devil, it is the risk of alienation. One profits to the extent that one is freed from the burdens of daily life—but the pact is a dangerous one. There is something Faustian about it. One must be careful.

I do not wish to exaggerate, because in reality things are not as simple as I would like to believe. As *The Divine Comedy* teaches us, temptations are contradictory. There is the temptation of a common future and the temptation of betrayal; the temptation to love and the temptation to hate; the temptation to generate and the temptation to destroy. Sometimes we can choose. Other times we bring a veritable storm upon ourselves.

What is certain—and this is what Dante exalted through the figure of Ulysses—is that we stand to lose everything; and yet, in accepting this insane wager, we can win everything. If devils are legion, temptations are a multitude of lives.

*T as in "*Terre*"—the land.*

The land is our condition. The land is beautiful because it is living. It produces, it nourishes, it quenches thirst. It is, all by itself, the infinite combination of the four fundamental elements of cosmology. Earth comes before matter and is the source of matter. One finds diamonds and oil in it, infinite riches; for me, it is also the abundance of the Po Valley, which yields several harvests a year. The land is therefore a foundation of matter, but also what we must work and transform in order to produce still more riches. The earth is nature transformed by labor: nothing is less natural than the earth of the Po Valley! There is not a single square centimeter that has not been transformed. It is a treasure that has been both received and reconstructed. In France I have had the same impression in Burgundy. The whole beauty of the land derives from this ambiguity: the land is at once the foundation of everything and the final product of human activity. In it one finds all the aspects of our relation to reality. Of course, I am speaking only of rich countries, which is unfair—I do not know poor countries very well. I now realize that I have always traveled, not in rich countries, but in countries where the land is generous. You know, labor and technology can make many poor lands rich. It is necessary to be daring. To be sure, there is an ecological balance that must be respected, and one must understand the necessary limits of development; but these concerns and these cautions cannot be allowed to clip the wings of the generosity with which man is capable of transforming the land, of enriching it through his labor. The ambiguity of the relationship between man and the land must be emphasized rather than eliminated: emphasized in full knowledge of the facts, which is to say with extreme caution.

But T is also the double T of "Twin Towers."

When the towers collapsed, we suddenly realized how much they were part of our imagination, and therefore of our life—I was about to say of our land. It is a little like the old tales in which a terrible storm destroys the entire harvest in ten minutes. When the Huns, one of the first barbarian tribes, invaded Italy, it was said that the grass would never grow again in the Po Valley. Farmers there repeat this prophecy still today—it has become a proverb for warding off misfortune. I don't know why, I'm obsessed with the idea that wealth will never grow again at Ground Zero. Last summer, before the attack on the towers, I was reading Gregorovius on the decadence of imperial Rome and the destruction of its landscape and architecture at the beginning of the papal Middle Ages. The barbarians were constantly at the gates, attacking and looting the Eternal City: Gregorovius laid special emphasis on the struggles within the papacy, the struggles between the old and new princes. When I saw the Twin Towers collapse, my first feeling was one of horror, then of pity: I realized that the violence of the conflict between those who were vying for control over imperial power had

TEMPTATION

become truly terrifying. Gregorovius added that the barbarian attacks gave birth to Roman archaeology. Might it be that the destruction of the towers of New York marks the beginning of an American archaeology?

In any case it must be understood that what happened is part of Empire. I know it is difficult to imagine, but even the murderous madness of al-Qaeda is part of Empire. For the moment, of course, the powerful are able to shape the world situation and use it to confirm their own power: we have entered into the Byzantine period of Empire. What is now being constructed on the ruins of the Twin Towers is an absolute Empire against the specters of evil. The skies, having been darkened by the dust of destruction, are now clouded by the wrath of a power that forgets the need for peace and democracy. Contrary to what I am supposed to have said or believe, I have no sympathy either for al-Qaeda or for fundamentalist and anti-American movements. But the real problem lies elsewhere, because I don't believe that a real alternative is available to us, a genuine choice among camps—for the time being, at least, we find ourselves in Empire. On the other hand, I feel an enormous sense of nostalgia for the Twin Towers, because those towers were the symbol of hope, progress, and work for all those who arrived in Manhattan. I hate the terrorism that destroyed the Twin Towers and the thousands of people who inhabited them during the day. I hate the terrorism that destroys tolerance and multiculturality, destroys the dreams of hybridity that we continue to associate with the United States and the hope for a new world—a new York. But I hate just as much the terror of a state that swears vengeance, that feeds terrorism by practicing terror itself, and that refuses to think politically because the use of violence—which is to say the institution of a state of generalized war—is easier to manage from the point of view of the authorities. For heaven's sake, the United States used to be something quite different! I find the American government today absolutely frightening.

U AS IN . . .

U as in Unity.

"One" is the principle of negation—the negation of all singularities, of all pluralities. One is empty abstraction. One is also the principle of theology, teleology, eugenics—none of these things has anything to do with unity. Terrified by the perverse consequences of this kind of thought, philosophers sometimes look to weaken its metaphysical implications by interpreting the idea of unity as an interaction of singularities. But this is a mystification: so long as One dominates concepts—no matter what form this domination assumes—it will dominate things, erase differences, kill singularities. One is the enemy.

Surely the concept of unity cannot be completely harmful?

It is important to distinguish between unity seen as a process of unification and unity conceived as an abstract bloc, that is, as "One." When unity is conceived in terms of action it is an ontological practice. Like any other action, unity implies a language. This language, like any other language, implies a multiplicity, which, like any other multiplicity, implies a "common." It is therefore not unity that is the opposite of multiplicity, but One. One is the principle of all alienation and imposes itself as negation. Negation is not action—it is a kind of gaping or gap, a nothingness. It is the principle of subtraction.

The multitude, then, is not One but unity?

The multitude as a set of singularities can be recognized as unity only in action. But its action is itself a proliferation of singularities. The only unity that the multitude can attain consists in the recognition of the common. But if, within the multitude, the common is only the construction of a common way of acting, then unity will also be common. And perhaps in that case it would be better no longer to speak of unity, to avoid giving the impression that the common is something organic. The common is living labor, and therefore the only unity possible.

V AS IN . . .

V as in Venice.

Venice is a sort of vice. There you are obliged to become as beautiful as your surroundings, to speak an exceptionally musical language, to continually nourish the senses with an omnipresent beauty. There is always a breeze that caresses you. And, then, of course, there is the water. Venice is at once the water of the maternal womb and the ultimate in artifice: a town fashioned by men to be able to live together, to be able to construct a community—a perfect universe.

I lived in Venice from 1963 until 1971. It is there that my first two children were born and there that I experienced 1968. It was not so much a refuge as a point of departure. It was from Venice that I ventured into the world.

How did the events of May 1968 unfold in Venice?

Nineteen sixty-eight was marvelous, because in reality it had begun long before: the school of architecture at the university there had been a center of student resistance since 1965. This was a truly fine department, very distinguished, and there were a number of very important artists who lived in the city during this period as well. And you had only to cross a few bridges before you came to dry land and the largest petrochemical complex in Italy, Porto Marghera. This is where I started out as an activist.

What was your role?

Since the early 1960s I had made militant political speeches aimed at raising people's awareness of their working conditions and defending their right to unionize. In 1963 we began to form grassroots committees and then organized the first large strike. In 1968 students from Venice and Padua joined forces with the workers at Porto Marghera. This worked out quite smoothly because they had been in constant contact for a decade: the school of architecture was a gathering place for the working class. And the intellectuals of Venice—led by the musician Luigi Nono and the painter Emilio Vedova—gave their wholehearted support to the movement. In June 1968 we blocked the opening of the famous art exposition, the Biennale—it finally took place three months later after being moved to another location! In September we disrupted the film festival, the "Mostra." It was an incredible mess! The police created a militarized zone by placing a small bomb in the Lido—the kind of the thing they used to do when they didn't know what to do to block protests: you could see through it. Two years later there were the events of August 1, 1970, the first day of summer vacation, again at Porto Marghera. Normally all the traffic in the northeast of Italy has to pass through the industrial zone: both cars and trains go right by the chemical factories. If you block the roads and the railroad tracks the region is totally paralyzed. Barricades were put up everywhere in the surrounding villages to prevent German tourists from getting through on their way to the south. A freight train was set on fire just outside Venice, right in the middle of everything. This was one of the most incredible things I have seen in my life—and God knows I've seen some incredible things! I laugh about it today, but the climate at Porto Marghera was often one of extreme violence: two kilometers from the most beautiful city in the world hundreds of workers were dying of cancer, literally poisoned by their work.

You stayed in Venice for two more years after May 1968.

Yes, and then I went to Milan. From a political point of view Milan was a much more important city than Venice. This was when I began to organize at Alfa Romeo, the largest car factory in the city. A committee had already been set up at Fiat in Turin, followed by ones at Pirelli, Siemens, all the great Milanese companies. In 1971–72 we launched what became *Autonomia Operaia* (Worker Autonomy)—at the time we still called ourselves *Potere Operaio* (Worker Power). Later we decided to dissolve this group in order to create a whole network of small structures throughout the region, building on our experience of collective management. Milan became the center of this experiment in autonomy.

How long did the experiment last?

Until our arrest. We thought that the worst of the crisis had already passed. In 1977 there had been a series of major confrontations in Italy, with enormous student demonstrations in Bologna, followed by a very violent wave of repression. We all thought that something very serious might happen, but as it turned out nothing did. On April 7, 1979, which is to say the day of the raid that sent us to prison, we were caught by surprise— no one any longer suspected such a thing might occur.

You really didn't see it coming?

No. I'd been afraid of being arrested several times before, but in 1979 everything seemed calm. And I certainly didn't expect that I would be arrested on the charge of having assassinated Moro! When I heard the charges against me I was staggered. It was absolutely unimaginable.

You said earlier that it was a "penitent" who cleared you of these charges.

On December 21, 1979 the authorities obtained the confession of a "penitent" who accused me of things that were altogether different from what they had initially believed. They freed him and kept me in prison: a new bill of indictment was substituted for the old one. The new charges were for the most part as absurd as the first ones; but at least I was no longer held responsible for the Moro affair, which was something. Neither the Right nor the Left objected—it was in the interest of both to be able to criminalize a social and political movement that had fought for its ideals for more than ten years, by identifying it with the marginal phenomenon of terrorism—because no matter what anyone may say today, terrorism during this decade of struggles was politically marginal.

You were defended by legal counsel?

Yes, I had terrific lawyers, Spazzali in Italy and Kiejman in France, as well as the support of an international committee. A number of prominent lawyers in Paris offered their assistance. Badinter couldn't defend me because he had just been appointed Minister of Justice, but we corresponded. There were friends, academic colleagues, and many others who helped out.

What, then, did the Italian "terrorism" of the 1970s amount to? Today we are told that we are at war against terrorism. Did your movement in any way resemble the terrorism we face today?

No, I don't believe there is any resemblance at all. The terrorism related to the class struggle was never nihilistic. It was more a form of political extremism that sometimes transformed struggles in the factories and political protest into armed actions. In general the terrorism of the 1970s was—with, alas, a few exceptions—a continuation of politics by other means. There are some who have wished to see this type of behavior as a "hyper-critical deviation," which is to say at once an antisystematic out-look and an attitude of distrust: a stance of rejection that renounces mediation—including the mediation of conflict—with other social actors. It is obvious that this definition is a bit facile since it corresponds simply to the definition of the work-ing class; one must really be obtuse to regard it as a deviation. I say to myself sometimes that it is a little bit as if a new genera-tion of anti-Dreyfusards were attacking Zola again. And it really is a shame that this antisystematic, hypercritical, deviant move-ment finally managed to destroy the totalitarian systems of colo-nialism, imperialism, and true socialism! These stupid people who still today go on speaking of the 1970s as a decade of ter-rorism are historically blind. They shift the level of confronta-tion from a political clash of desires, which is to say a set of struggles that sought to produce life, to a clash of cultures, of civilizations, in which the rigid defense of identity prevents any critical discourse. The terrorism one finds today is an identity-based nihilism, a destructive apologia of identity and closure. In any case this is what we now find ourselves faced with—because it is, alas, the form assumed by the conflict among various impe-rial elites, each of which seeks to impose its will upon the others.

W AS IN . . .

W as in Wittgenstein.

Wittgenstein represents one of the great philosophical turning points of the century. We've already spoken of Heidegger. Wittgenstein is the "other"—the other great lineage of contemporary thought, the one that destroyed once and for all the notion that there is a simple relationship between sign and reality. He used the sign to reconquer reality. But the most important thing is not the process by which the sign is related to reality, but the community of the sign and reality in language. With Wittgenstein there was an extraordinary rediscovery of a phenomenology of passions within language—the insight that, beyond language, living labor and the affects produce reality.

This is something that really moved me when I read Wittgenstein for the first time. And that made me want to do philosophy, which wasn't the case with Heidegger!

When you speak of passion within language, what do you mean?

With Wittgenstein, language becomes the condition of the mind, its very form. He introduced us to an analysis of language in which it is not the philosophical questioning that counts, but rather the linguistic form of the question, the intonation of the voice, all the bodily elements of language that are now seen to be central. This was extraordinary. And this technique made it possible to reexamine a whole series of problems—private language, suffering, certain moral problems. The linguistic turn was not a minor revolution: it was a total upheaval. Afterward, to a large extent, the rift between Continental philosophy and Anglo-Saxon philosophy prevented us from understanding how strong Wittgenstein's influence had been on Continental philosophy itself. I think that Continental philosophy would be unthinkable today without the Wittgensteinian heritage.

It is rather bizarre that, in France, foreign philosophers are never read in their "pure" state—by the time they arrive they've already been reinterpreted. Thus there was, for example, a first Heidegger who arrived with Sartre, but it was necessary to wait another fifty years until access could be had to the true Heidegger. In much the same way, Wittgenstein was first read on account of the interest in language stirred up by Lacan. The idea that one must undergo psychoanalysis in order to read German philosophy is quite remarkable. Lacan did to Wittgenstein exactly what Sartre did to Heidegger, with the result that reading Wittgenstein today on his own terms is an arduous enterprise. This phenomenon of translation/betrayal is very frequently encountered in France. Think of the importance of Maine de Biran, or of Kojève and Hyppolite, for Hegel: three very great commentators who were at the same time responsible for a very partial and biased reception of the original work.

Do you think that Wittgenstein's thought remains important today?

I think that Wittgenstein, much more than Heidegger, was the one who enabled us to enter into the postmodern. The postmodern is dominated by immaterial production, a form of production that has now spread to every area of life. The reading of this world obliges us to follow Wittgenstein, particularly with regard to his interpretation of language as the constitutive movement of being—as sign, as articulation, as structure. At the same time there is something Heideggerian in Wittgenstein, because this structure of language is given: it is there. It traces a veritable ontological horizon, an ontological foundation.

The centrality of Wittgenstein's thought has to do with the fact that he took language as the fundamental term of analysis in order to understand the nature of the body. The body therefore becomes a linguistic process. From this perspective, Wittgenstein can be seen to be more important than his neo-Kantian predecessors because, even when they made the symbolic a central element, they always reduced it to a formal horizon. Wittgenstein, on the other hand, speaks of being, of bodies, and the way in which bodies put themselves in contact with each other by communicating their feelings and intentions. Even the hermeneutic philosophy of someone like Gadamer is vulnerable to the sort of objections that can be brought against neo-Kantianism and/or epistemological formalism. Gadamer's philosophy remains forever stuck in the nineteenth century. My first thesis was on Dilthey and Weber—perhaps this is why I react so strongly to certain philosophical positions.

Are you still interested in Dilthey?

In Dilthey, yes, but not in Gadamer. I find that with Gadamer one loses the ontological dimension. Dilthey was a product of the German thought of the 1870s, and from there a very clear line of descent can be traced down to Heidegger. I don't think this is true of Gadamer—at any rate this is what I tried to show in my thesis. The attempt to characterize Continental philosophy in terms of the hermeneutic approach is often a sign that the old historicism is at work: academics delight in this sort of thing because it legitimizes quite brilliant work in the history of philosophy. But for me philosophy is something else.

And Ricoeur?

Ricoeur is a somewhat unusual figure, an outsider whose heterodox brand of phenomenology allows him to move all around. Paradoxically, even though he has developed his thinking within the doctrine of interpretation, I don't think he can be regarded as a practitioner of hermeneutics. He is willing to live in the world of language, in reality, in the being of language. One finds moments of extreme modernity in his work, and an exceptional critical capacity, a capacity for identification, an understanding of the processes that underlie different cultural positions. I have always considered Ricoeur more as an exceptionally acute cultural critic than a truly original philosopher—even though I am perfectly aware that in saying this I am being unfair, because some of his works are absolutely remarkable. Just the same, in France, if one takes away the three monsters—Foucault, Deleuze, Derrida—who's left?

Levinas?

No. On the other hand, someone who is important and who must be reread is Merleau-Ponty, especially in the late writings after 1952–53. Merleau-Ponty understood the link that exists between the body, power, and language—an impressive anticipation. But when one doesn't confine oneself to translation/betrayal, one is barred from academic philosophy. Merleau-Ponty has been collapsed into Sartre, erasing a whole part of an extraordinary philosophical career that prefigured the work of Foucault and Deleuze. Merleau-Ponty is a tremendous philosopher.

Twentieth-century philosophy really began with three monsters: Bergson, Gentile,[15] and Husserl. These three philosophers

---

15. Giovanni Gentile (1875-1944) is remembered chiefly for his reinterpretation of Hegelian thought, which rapidly came to dominate academic Italian philosophy. An early supporter of fascism, he became Minister of Education in Mussolini's first cabinet in 1922, and in this capacity carried out a far-reaching

represented the best of the French, Italian, and German traditions. Each of them synthesized the dynamic elements of nineteenth-century bourgeois thought. It was the apogee of bourgeois philosophy, a golden age notable for its ability to seize the past and project it into the future. But the war of 1914–1918 marked the end of this period and signaled the onset of decadence. Heidegger perfectly embodied this decadence from the 1920s onward. With Wittgenstein there was a brief flurry of resistance against the corruption of the age: the linguistic turn was the reflection of a full-blown crisis. Wittgenstein's work, in relation to Heideggerian thought, represents a radical shift of ontological inquiry. Merleau-Ponty emerged in the same type of philosophical context as Wittgenstein and introduced a corporeal point of view: a "bottom-up" approach directed against all philosophies of totality. Merleau-Ponty performed the same maieutic operation on corporeality that Wittgenstein had performed on language. Both provided the essential elements for constructing a philosophy of postmodernity.

Nonetheless I think that the body remains a great unknown for philosophy. It's interesting that you bring up Merleau-Ponty, for he really did try to capture that aspect from the point of view of phenomenology, within the domain of the visible. At the same time, this philosophy of the visible and the body wasn't really accepted.

---

program of educational reform and reorganization that forms the basis of the school system in Italy still today. He was assassinated in April 1944 by Communist partisans.

It wasn't accepted at the time, but twenty years later or so it was, owing to the attempt by Foucault—and, to a lesser extent, Deleuze—to subjectivize the body. The difficult thing is to speak of it using the right terms: there is always a risk of falling back into a materialist empiricism or an almost spiritualist vitalism. To speak of the body is above all a problem of language. The philosophical tradition that originated with the Greeks of dividing the body in two has proved difficult to escape! It was Popper who spoke of the poverty of philosophy and of the necessity of being anti-Platonist—but he certainly didn't succeed in this himself. Still I would very much like to organize a philosophical society, a kind of *Collège de philosophie* devoted to the body, whose members would never utter the words *spirit, soul, substantial unity, entelechy,* or any other terms that, even when they unify, nonetheless imply an ontological separation. This is why it is so important to consider the body as an agent of intelligent production. Because what the separation of body and soul really signifies is that the spirit dominates the body. Society was therefore structured in this way as well: the soul commanded and the body obeyed. This was the order and the measure of social hierarchy and production. If, however, one reverses these terms and says that production is made not by the soul but by the body (which is not a new idea, since reproduction has always been a function of the body), if the reappropriation of intellectual force is situated in the body, then the body becomes the unit of production and reproduction. The whole separation between the corporeal and the spiritual, this whole religious view that the body must be made to disappear—all that vanishes.

What a clever idea it was, just the same, to say that the soul is eternal and the body mortal! From the point of view of power, it was a stroke of genius. The paradox is that Christianity never said this: the great dogma of the resurrection of the body runs completely contrary to it. It's not only the eschatological aspect that interests me, even though this is a very important element of the story, but is also the rediscovery of a materialist religion. There are many other elements: the Eucharist, for example, which represents the material transmission of the flesh of God through the host and wine. The resurrection of the body is obviously the most important thing from the point of view of physical materialism. Perhaps I will wind up one day working on this problem. Today, the discourse about the body is linked to the discourse about metamorphosis. This is the other great line of thought that affirms the importance and centrality of the body. It is a mark of the singularity that is associated with the metamorphosis of man into God, of God into man, of man into Nature. These are often rather contradictory forms, but if you read Ovid's *Metamorphoses* it becomes possible to appreciate how important this transformation of the body is in man's thinking. In one of my writings I called classical antiquity the "age of the centaur," because the confusion between man and nature at that time was total. Metamorphosis is thus a happy, simple, direct form of reciprocity. In the modern era, which is to say the age of "*Homo homo*," the idea of metamorphosis began to change: it became the magic dividing line between the forces of nature and intellectual and political innovation, lying at the heart of a dream of transformation. In the contemporary era, now that technology completely determines the relation between man and machine, technology has placed itself in the service of desire. This is an enormous transformation: we can now modify man, causing the dream of metamorphosis to cross over from utopia to science. And a whole path that remains yet to be discovered opens up before us. . . .

X AS IN . . .

X as in x—the unknown of an equation. In order to think of our time and its multiple metamorphoses, we therefore have to think with one or more unknowns.

It is obvious that a thousand problems present themselves today. Physical prostheses, genetic engineering, the relation between the body and the machine, the machine as cybernetics—all these things, as I was saying, sketch a path to be traveled with caution, but traveled nonetheless all the way to the end. And we will be able to do this only once we have first recomposed the image of the body in every discipline, in medicine, in engineering, in philosophy, in biology. This transversal operation constitutes a truly profound postmodern revolution. But such an operation can give rise to unforeseen things, and one of these things is the monster (in the sense in which I employ this term).

One comes back, then, to a problem that has already been posed a thousand times: this epochal metamorphosis that we are presently experiencing, where the relation between nature and culture has been completely internalized, where the relation between a project of life and technological progress in the reproduction of life has become central. I don't know how things will eventually turn out. This x of the unknown in mathematics is the unforeseen, the unhoped for. The unforeseen is, by definition, that which may happen. The monstrous hybridization that is occurring everywhere in our cultures, our languages, and our cities certainly displays an incredible creativity; but the negative effects are so great that we are frightened by our own capacity for creation. The ambiguity is quite obviously profound, but we can't go backward: the problem is there, right before our eyes. Faced with this x, with this unknown, no fundamentalist retreat is possible: flight into New Age religions will not ease our discomfort. The greatest danger is pretending to see nothing. Only the invention and practice of a new democracy of the multitude will be able to save us from catastrophe. We need a biopolitical democracy equal to the monster that looms before us.

Y AS IN . . .

Y as in Yet.

Eyes—the gaze—represent anticipation as well as an attachment to the past and blindness: anticipation of that which is yet to come.

The eye is also par excellence *the eye of the artist—the eye of one who "knows" how to see.*

One of the most disturbing phenomena today is the tendency of everyone to suppose that he or she is an artist. Everyone thinks he or she is able to see beyond the surface of the world around us. One must not confuse a genuinely intelligent and corporeal capacity—which is to say a passionate intensity, a steadfastness of will, a vocation to confront reality—with the random little fantasies that one has every day, if only there's a little sunshine. . . .

I say that because, when it's sunny, I often see spots that impair my vision! Debord always used to say, "If you want to see, go to the cinema!" He had in mind all those people who seek truth through intuition, and answered them like the rationalist snob he was: watch a movie if you wish to "see." The problem is not seeing, but constructing in order to know. Debord meant that it is necessary to construct an ideal type through which reality can be explored. In Deleuze and Guattari there is a similar idea: the construction of a man who is able to fly over reality, to survey reality. It's rather curious, because their attitude was very different than Debord's rationalism, but the notion of an overview is the same. What do the eyes allow us to see? In what dimension? In order to see one must have the necessary tools—tools that operate within the gaze, that help to problematize the gaze, that make it a questioning of the world, of its power, its drives, its tendencies. This is what I was trying to get at when I brought up Job. In analyzing this gaze upon the world there is a danger of setting oneself up as a prophet: false prophets lead only to a sort of general nihilism, an annihilation that ends up causing them to be forgotten in their turn. To question the world is to invent it at each instant, but there is in this a constructive dimension that is quite the opposite of prophetic nihilism.

In nihilism there is something very denying—

It is the mystical aspect of nihilism that bothers me. From this perspective, even the ideal type that Debord speaks of and the

overview described by Deleuze and Guattari seem to me to bor-
der on this mystical type of attitude, because in effect one has
reintroduced a form of transcendence, a supra-historical point
of view.

Z AS IN . . .

Z as in Zeno.

Zeno of Elea is associated, of course, with paradoxes—ones that all premodern and postmodern materialists must confront, with the exception of Spinoza. Generally speaking, these paradoxes have to do with the impossibility of considering atoms otherwise than in respect of their separation; the impossibility of considering life otherwise than as a series of passive arrangements. They represent the reactionary translation of a revolutionary materialism. Materialism, in and of itself, is a formidable instrument of struggle against all forms of authoritarian preconstitution, in the domain of science no less than in religion, in social life, in the practice of political theory. The problem is that once this model of authoritarian preconstitution has been destroyed there is no getting out from under it. Thus Zeno: a suicide of reason—a futile suicide, because the premises on which his thought is founded are futile.

Time is the rupture between continuity and discontinuity: it is something that begins at each instant. When one takes a line made up of points and proceeds to divide these points ad infinitum, it isn't a question of catching up with the tortoise but of hurling oneself into the void. This is what time is: if one throws oneself into the void, one overtakes the tortoise. Zeno stands for the reactionary, pessimistic, violently negative aspect of philosophies of time and of Being. Zeno looks at the world analytically, from the outside—outside action. But it would be false to believe that an analytical necessity exists that always leads us to look at the world, and the things that make it up, a posteriori. To the contrary, one is always operating within an inductive mechanism, a dynamic mechanics; and this dynamic is dominated by the body, which is to say by the passions—by the organization and arrangement of their intensity, by the continuity of behaviors, by the leap that one makes into reality.

It is absolutely necessary to leap into reality—to plunge into it, to rush into it—because this is the only way to change the world. Life is just this: changing the world, transforming it, inventing it. Revolutionizing it. And yet what a price I have had to pay in order to begin again to construct it! Today my return is accomplished, I can forget Zeno's paradoxes once and for all. I walk a great deal now. To return is to begin to walk again: to find a way out from all impasses; also—and above all—to revive passions that had been crushed by failure. This means fewer memories and more new experiences. The future doesn't have an old heart. The future is something that we construct every day, and that for this reason is always new. To begin again is not a matter of going backward again, of endlessly cutting up and dividing the episodes of life—as Zeno did with space and time. It is a matter of relying on the past. It is the rediscovery of the beginning. We are communists from the beginning; but the beginning is the present act. Communism is the future. I have a normal life.

INDEX